SEXUAL VALUES

OPPOSING VIEWPOINTS®

SEXUAL VALUES

OPPOSING VIEWPOINTS®

David L. Bender & Bruno Leone, *Series Editors*

Lisa Orr, *Book Editor*

OPPOSING VIEWPOINTS SERIES ®

Greenhaven Press, Inc.   PO Box 289009   San Diego, CA 92128-9009

Library of Congress Cataloging-in-Publication Data

Sexual values : opposing viewpoints / Lisa Orr, book editor.
    p.   cm. — (Opposing viewpoints series)
    Includes bibliographical references.
    Summary: Presents opposing viewpoints on such issues as the sexual revolution, homosexuality, sexual ethics, pornography, and sex education.
    ISBN 0-89908-420-6. — ISBN 0-89908-445-1 (lib. bdg.)
    1. Sexual ethics—United States. 2. Sex customs—United States. [1. Sexual ethics.] I. Orr, Lisa, 1966-   . II. Series.
HQ34.S48   1989
306.7'0973—dc20   89-36527
                                                               CIP
                                                               AC

"Congress shall make no law...
abridging the freedom of speech,
or of the press."

First Amendment to the US Constitution

The basic foundation of our democracy is the first amendment guarantee of freedom of expression. The *Opposing Viewpoints Series* is dedicated to the concept of this basic freedom and the idea that it is more important to practice it than to enshrine it.

Contents

Chapter 5: What Sexual Philosophy Is Best?

Why Consider Opposing Viewpoints?

The Importance of Examining Opposing Viewpoints

The purpose of the Opposing Viewpoints books, and this book in particular, is to present balanced, and often difficult to find, opposing points of view on complex and sensitive issues.

Probably the best way to become informed is to analyze the positions of those who are regarded as experts and well studied on issues. It is important to consider every variety of opinion in an attempt to determine the truth. Opinions from the mainstream of society should be examined. But also important are opinions that are considered radical, reactionary, or minority as well as those stigmatized by some other uncomplimentary label. An important lesson of history is the eventual acceptance of many unpopular and even despised opinions. The ideas of Socrates, Jesus, and Galileo are good examples of this.

Readers will approach this book with their own opinions on the issues debated within it. However, to have a good grasp of one's own viewpoint, it is necessary to understand the arguments of those with whom one disagrees. It can be said that those who do not completely understand their adversary's point of view do not fully understand their own.

A persuasive case for considering opposing viewpoints has been presented by John Stuart Mill in his work *On Liberty*. When examining controversial issues it may be helpful to reflect on this suggestion:

> The only way in which a human being can make some approach to knowing the whole of a subject, is by hearing what can be said about it by persons of every variety of opinion, and studying all modes in which it can be looked at by every character of mind. No wise man ever acquired his wisdom in any mode but this.

Analyzing Sources of Information

The Opposing Viewpoints books include diverse materials taken from magazines, journals, books, and newspapers, as well as statements and position papers from a wide range of individuals, organizations and governments. This broad spectrum of sources helps to develop patterns of thinking which are open to the consideration of a variety of opinions.

Pitfalls To Avoid

A pitfall to avoid in considering opposing points of view is that of regarding one's own opinion as being common sense and the most rational stance and the point of view of others as being only opinion and naturally wrong. It may be that another's opinion is correct and one's own is in error.

Another pitfall to avoid is that of closing one's mind to the opinions of those with whom one disagrees. The best way to approach a dialogue is to make one's primary purpose that of understanding the mind and arguments of the other person and not that of enlightening him or her with one's own solutions. More can be learned by listening than speaking.

It is my hope that after reading this book the reader will have a deeper understanding of the issues debated and will appreciate the complexity of even seemingly simple issues on which good and honest people disagree. This awareness is particularly important in a democratic society such as ours where people enter into public debate to determine the common good. Those with whom one disagrees should not necessarily be regarded as enemies, but perhaps simply as people who suggest different paths to a common goal.

Developing Basic Reading and Thinking Skills

In this book carefully edited opposing viewpoints are purposely placed back to back to create a running debate; each viewpoint is preceded by a short quotation that best expresses the author's main argument. This format instantly plunges the reader into the midst of a controversial issue and greatly aids that reader in mastering the basic skill of recognizing an author's point of view.

A number of basic skills for critical thinking are practiced in the activities that appear throughout the books in the series. Some of the skills are:

Evaluating Sources of Information   The ability to choose from among alternative sources the most reliable and accurate source in relation to a given subject.

Separating Fact from Opinion   The ability to make the basic distinction between factual statements (those that can be demonstrated or verified empirically) and statements of opinion (those that are beliefs or attitudes that cannot be proved).

Identifying Stereotypes The ability to identify oversimplified, exaggerated descriptions (favorable or unfavorable) about people and insulting statements about racial, religious or national groups, based upon misinformation or lack of information.

Recognizing Ethnocentrism   The ability to recognize attitudes or opinions that express the view that one's own race, culture, or group is inherently superior, or those attitudes that judge another culture or group in terms of one's own.

It is important to consider opposing viewpoints and equally important to be able to critically analyze those viewpoints. The activities in this book are designed to help the reader master these thinking skills. Statements are taken from the book's viewpoints and the reader is asked to analyze them. This technique aids the reader in developing skills that not only can be applied to the viewpoints in this book, but also to situations where opinionated spokespersons comment on controversial issues. Although the activities are helpful to the solitary reader, they are most useful when the reader can benefit from the interaction of group discussion.

Using this book and others in the series should help readers develop basic reading and thinking skills. These skills should improve the readers' ability to understand what they read. Readers should be better able to separate fact from opinion, substance from rhetoric and become better consumers of information in our media-centered culture.

This volume of the Opposing Viewpoints books does not advocate a particular point of view. Quite the contrary! The very nature of the book leaves it to the reader to formulate the opinions he or she finds most suitable. My purpose as publisher is to see that this is made possible by offering a wide range of viewpoints which are fairly presented.

David L. Bender
Publisher

Introduction

"Sex cannot be contained within a definition of physical pleasure, it cannot be understood as merely itself for it has stood for too long as a symbol of profound connection between human beings."

Elizabeth Janeway, *Between Myth and Morning*, 1974

As with most human values, sexual values have passed through periods of crests (times of liberalization) and troughs (times of conservatism or extreme reaction). In the sixties and seventies sexual values underwent significant change in America and throughout most of the Western world. Rigid sexual standards of the 1950s were replaced by what many viewed as unbridled permissiveness. As recently as forty years ago, certain values were given: sex should be confined to marriage, prostitution was unquestionably a crime, pornography was a moral blight and homosexuality, a depravity. However, studies revealed that during the sixties and seventies many people were defecting from these traditional values. According to the US Department of Commerce, the number of unmarried couples living together increased over 15 percent and the National Public Health Services reported that the percentage of babies born out of wedlock nearly doubled (399,000 to 666,000) from 1970 to 1980. Also by 1980, there were two million prostitutes in the US, with 600,000 of them 18 years of age or younger, while pornography sales increased to $4 billion annually. Finally, the protests and increased visibility of gays led to a definite liberalization in attitude toward homosexuality.

Many of these increasingly liberal sexual mores carried over into the 1980s. But new and virulent forms of sexually transmitted diseases such as herpes and chlamydia became the subject of media attention and dramatically influenced people's attitudes toward sex. In addition, AIDS has had the most significant impact, turning the "joy of sex" into the "fear of sex" in the minds and practices of many individuals and institutions. Whereas a return to earlier, more rigid sexual standards is possible, it seems unlikely. The question therefore is, what direction will sexual values take in the age of AIDS?

Sexual Values: Opposing Viewpoints addresses this and other weighty sexual issues facing the wary public. Replacing

13

Greenhaven's successful 1983 edition of the same title, it contains new viewpoints and introduces several new topics. The issues debated are, Have Sexual Values in America Changed? How Should Society Treat Homosexuality? Is Sex Education Beneficial? Is Pornography Harmful? and What Sexual Philosophy Is Best? As with all books in the Opposing Viewpoints Series, it takes no sides. Rather it leaves the authors themselves to debate the issues, and, more importantly, the reader to decide the outcome.

Have Sexual Values Changed in America?

SEXUAL VALUES

Chapter Preface

In a 1989 article, Robert Selverstone, psychologist and human sexuality teacher, reported asking his students' parents, "Do you find the prevailing sexual climate and sexual attitudes similar to, or different from, those that existed while you were growing up?" The parents responded that they had grown up in a sexual climate of "silence, embarrassment, ignorance, and fear." In contrast, they believed their children were growing up in a much more open society. The parents reported changes in their own attitudes as well. They pointed out that they were better able to talk to their children about sex. They also suggested that their children had better access to accurate information about sex.

Not everyone believes these new, open attitudes toward sex are beneficial. Many people are concerned that children are encouraged to experiment with premarital sex. They believe that the increased acceptance of premarital sexual activity is connected to the increase in teen pregnancy. Between 1970 and 1985, births to teenage mothers increased by 50 percent.

While most Americans agree that a change in sexual attitudes has occurred, few agree whether these changes are beneficial or harmful. The following chapter reflects this controversy.

"Sex has simply become more trouble than it's worth."

The Sexual Revolution Is Over

Susan Ager

In the following viewpoint, Susan Ager, a writer for Knight-Ridder News Service, argues that the sexual revolution is over. Ager blames AIDS, a preoccupation with work and getting ahead, and a new conservatism for the end of the revolution.

As you read, consider the following questions:

1. According to the author, how has sex changed since the 1960s?
2. In Ager's opinion, why is the end of the sexual revolution a relief to some?
3. How does Ager believe the media has contributed to the decline of sex?

Susan Ager, "Is Sex Too Big a Hassle Now?" *St. Paul Pioneer Press and Dispatch*, February 16, 1986. Reprinted with permission from Knight-Ridder Newspapers.

How long ago it seems, those days of wild abandon—see-through blouses and topless bathing suits, open marriages, nakedness in the mud at Woodstock, "Last Tango in Paris." "No one will be watching us," the Beatles sang in 1968. "Why don't we do it in the road?"

No one does it in the road, or in the mud, anymore. (Those who would do it there probably could not be trusted to make a commitment.) "If it feels good, do it" and "Love the one you're with"—the tallyhos of the Sexual Revolution—have been replaced by "Know your partner" and "Be careful."

In the '60s, we didn't worry about pregnancy. We had the magic Pill. Now, for many, the Pill is more feared than pregnancy, and other methods are either dangerous or annoying.

In the '60s, if we caught something, an injection would fix it. Now, we've learned some diseases are forever. We know sex can kill.

In the '60s, we all expected to grow richer and better and happier. We tossed away sexual taboos with gusto. We were free! Now we're working harder than ever to stay in place financially. Who has time or energy for sex anymore? Besides, it's all getting kind of old, if you know what we mean. How about a hug, honey, and let's get to sleep early?

Where's the Joy?

Whatever happened to the joy of sex anyhow?

No one challenges the value of intimacy, the buzzword of the '80s. But the signs are that, even wrapped in the warm glow of affection, sex ain't what it used to be.

For singles, intimacy with strangers is dancing in the dark: Is he bisexual? Can I get AIDS from doing this? Who's she been with? If I give him herpes, will he still love me? Is he telling me the truth? Should I tell her?

For two-career couples, especially those with children, good sex is for special occasions. On other days, it's the last thing before blissful sleep, tucked quickly between the brushing of teeth and the snoring. "I'm so-o-o-o tired" has replaced "I have a headache," but it's no lie.

Seduced by success, men and especially women are finding psychic orgasms in boardrooms rather than physical ones in bedrooms.

What's the Use?

Taunted by media images of passion—sleek and dramatic and totally fulfilling—many singles and spouses conclude they can't keep up. They are capable, they sadly conclude, of only one orgasm per night, and sometimes that one must be eked out. For many, sex has simply become more trouble than it's worth.

"When I started work in this field (16 years ago), there was an extreme enthusiasm (for sex) and a looking for more pleasure, to get more out of sex," said psychologist Sallie Schumacher, president of the American Association of Sex Educators, Counselors and Therapists.

"There still is that—even to an unrealistic degree—but . . . many people (are) just backing away, with the attitude of 'What's the use?' People are a little bit let down." . . .

Ed Gamble. Reprinted with permission.

"The revolution is over," *Time* magazine proclaimed in 1984, remarking on the sudden wisdom and maturity of those who had concluded that monogamy felt better than sleeping around.

What happened to it? We believed those who promised that if only we let our long-repressed sexuality free, it would fulfill us and make us happy. We indulged; we overindulged. We were fooled, or we fooled ourselves.

Consider an analogy made by Dr. Marshall Shearer, an Ann Arbor, Mich., psychiatrist who remembers protests of the '60s at which University of Michigan students demanded what they called their "f-----g rights"—open dormitories.

"If we liken sex to a sense of humor," Shearer's analogy goes, "then most everybody has a sense of humor, and most everybody has sex. What is the value system people use in their humor? Some people don't like ethnic jokes. Some people like puns; others don't. . . . How does someone use their sexuality? Is it to produce orgasms, to prove a sense of sexual attractiveness? Is it for power?

"Because the physical aspects of sex were under wraps for so long, when those aspects were brought into the open, people went for the 'Big O,' male and female. Now, they're finding the Big O is, by itself, not as full as they thought it was. They need love or commitment, the psychological intimacy to go with the physical intimacy.

"We've found out that yes, we can produce the most laughter by tickling somebody," Shearer said, but it's not nearly as satisfying as the laughter from a shared reminiscence over breakfast with someone you love. "Yes," he continued, "we can produce big orgasms with vibrators or the right technique, but it's not as satisfying as commitment."

Everyone agrees that happened even before herpes, and ultimately AIDS, dealt the death blow to casual sex, making it seem, as one Detroit bachelor put it, "like social suicide."

Sighs of relief can be heard across the land. Feeling social pressure to be more sexual than they wanted to be, some people can now smartly cite their fear of AIDS as a reason for saying no.

Why the Apathy?

Others, for whom sexual pleasure has dipped despite their best efforts, are looking for help. Therapists who specialize in family and sexual issues say as many as 75 percent of their clients complain of disinterest in sex.

The American Psychiatric Association considers it an official diagnosis: Inhibited Sexual Desire (ISD), a.k.a. "sexual apathy" or "sexual anorexia." Starving oneself in the midst of plenty.

Dr. Harold Lief, who led an American Psychiatric Association investigation into ISD, estimates 20 percent of Americans suffer from desire problems for a smorgasbord of reasons—fatigue, resentment, anger, depression, preoccupation with work, illness, fear.

The irony is pathetic. Having finally learned exactly how to do it, some people are enjoying it less. Having learned the steps to the dance, they can no longer hear the music.

Drowning in Sex

"The media have cheapened sex," shrugged a 33-year-old Grosse Pointe financial adviser, who has been divorced for six years and who has concluded that sex is a tired substitute for love.

"The media image doesn't deal with birth control. It doesn't deal with hormonal swings. It doesn't deal with the differences between men and women," he said.

Neither does it deal with insecurities, sexually transmitted diseases, various physical problems that stymie free sexual expression or the real-life ebb and flow of passion in a committed couple's life.

Who burps in the movies? When does the smoke alarm ever go off? What would happen if Richard Gere got a leg cramp at the moment Debra Winger would least sympathize with his pain?

The images are high-gloss versions of what real sex is like. But despite their falsity, they are everywhere. We are now drowning in sex, rather than being nourished by it, and perhaps that is part of the problem. . . .

A few "sexperts" even wonder aloud if sex was ever meant to be fun, a question as boggling as wondering how the universe began.

The Pendulum Swings

Sexual satisfaction for some comes down to the economic principle of supply and demand: The price of an item is high if the demand is high and the supply is low. If the supply far exceeds demand, the item becomes cheap.

Said Fran Lebowitz, a best-selling author: "Only teen-agers and middle-aged people expect a lot out of sex, because they are having the least. People who are having the most sex, they know it's not what it's cracked up to be."

No More Whoopie

It sure looks as if the sexual revolution is over. Who won? Who knows? All I know is that what the sensual Bob Eubanks so charmingly calls "whoopie" has gone the way of the hula hoop, disco and the money market. Sex in the 1980s is kind of like Oklahoma: rich in potential resources, bleak to look at.

Ian Shoales, *Mademoiselle*, August 1987.

Helen Gurley Brown, editor of *Cosmopolitan* magazine and a longtime proponent of recreational sex, responded this way when asked if sex can ever be fun again:

"The pendulum always swings, and no matter how boring sex may seem right now, because it's so available and so supersudsy clean, and it's about as forbidden as cottage cheese and grapefruit. The pendulum swings. It has throughout history, if we'll just be a little patient. Repression will probably sweep upon us again, and sex will be just as forbidden and naughty and racy and exciting as it ever was."

"The . . . sexual revolution continues despite the growing belief that the sexual behavior of Americans has become more conservative."

The Sexual Revolution Is Continuing

Michael Ross

Michael Ross is the editor of *Youthwalk*, a religious magazine for teenagers. In the following viewpoint, he argues that the sexual revolution is still going strong. Even the threat of AIDS, he writes, has not affected the sexual behavior of singles. Ross argues that in addition to being unwise, this behavior is unhealthy and immoral.

As you read, consider the following questions:

1. According to the author, how has AIDS affected singles?
2. What is wrong with the "Ethic of Intimacy," in the author's opinion?
3. How does Ross believe the 1980s will be remembered?

Michael Ross, "The Sexual Revolution Is Continuing," *Eternity*, January 1989. Reprinted by permission of *Eternity* Magazine; Copyright © 1989, Foundation for Christian Living, c/o 1716 Spruce Street, Philadelphia, PA 19103.

W ere a future civilization to one day unearth the telltale ruins of present-day America, it would undoubtedly conclude we spent a third of our time having sex, another third planning it, and the other third talking about it," writes author Randy Alcorn in his book *Christians in the Wake of the Sexual Revolution*.

Newspapers in Los Angeles publish invitations for homosexual partners. A sex shop in New York City sells more than 46 films and videos that feature bestiality of every type. Rows of pornographic tabloids line city streets in Chicago.

Prostitutes, massage parlors, adult book stores, strip joints, gay baths, singles bars—they've become as much a part of urban America as freeways and skyscrapers.

After 20 years, the so-called sexual revolution continues despite the growing belief that the sexual behavior of Americans has become more conservative.

Keeping It Casual

Studies indicate that, while most Americans are concerned about the spread of AIDS and other sexually transmitted diseases (STDs), single men and women—age 20-39—aren't willing to give up casual sex.

A survey of 12,000 single men and women, conducted in 1986 by New York research psychologist Srully Blotnick, shows a decline in the approval of recreational sex since the freewheeling '60s. However, Blotnick's findings point out that a majority of young Americans are still very open-minded about sex and don't oppose premarital intercourse. A less extensive survey conducted that same year by *USA Today*, found that out of 999 college students from 104 campuses across the nation, 60 percent said they were unwilling to give up casual sex in spite of the threat of AIDS.

A study reported in *The New York Times* indicates that cases of some little known but worrisome venereal diseases have increased. Among the better-known venereal diseases, the number of syphilis cases is creeping up after five years of decline and gonorrhea strains that resist antibiotics represent a growing proportion of the 800,000 cases of that disease reported annually.

This current spread of diseases associated with unprotected sexual acts and promiscuity is alarming to health officials because of the associated heightened risk of AIDS.

Although Americans appear to be more accepting of traditional values, a closer look shows sexual morality in this country is still in decline, and the sexual attitudes of younger Americans are signficantly lower than of the older generation.

Tim Stafford, author of three Christian books on teen sexuality and contributing editor to *Campus Life* magazine, says Americans have passed through one phase of the sexual revolution: the period when the "Playboy Ethic" ruled. Stafford believes our society is now entering a phase that promotes what he calls the "Ethic of Intimacy"—a set of values about sex that still strays from biblical standards.

"It's not the same as traditional morality," Stafford says, "although, in some circumstances, it may have some common ground. But it is really saying 'Sex is a very significant and sacred expression of love and it ought to be saved for moments of real intimacy between two people.'"

He says the problem with this mode of thought is that there is really no operational definition of what intimacy is, and it ends up being very much like the Playboy ethic.

Changes in the Wrong Direction

"According to this way of thinking, 'If it feels good, then you can say it feels intimate.' You end up seeing an awful lot of people who are involved with each other sexually who are really kidding themselves about the level of intimacy in their relationship," Stafford says. "To them, their behavior is sanctioned because they feel intimate with the other person. Couples today say things like, 'We're planning on getting married.' Well, point of fact is that they almost never do."

Far from Dead

Though it seems AIDS has had some effect on sex practices, the sexual revolution is far from dead. . . . Trends . . . do not picture a sexual climate of conservatism and traditional values as some have been predicting. People are spending more of their lives unmarried. Along with this has come increasing acceptance, even expectation, of sex outside of marriage.

Michael Bennett and Rebecca Bennett, *The Plain Truth*, April 1989.

Stafford points to a *Cosmopolitan* magazine survey in which they asked their readers, whom Stafford considers sexually loose, how their behavior had changed.

"The women who answered said that they had changed their behavior quite a bit. It turns out (where as before many would go to bed on the first date), now they would wait until the third date. Well, that's a change, but it isn't in exactly the right direction." . . .

Breaking Down Society

The '80s could very well be remembered as the decade of the war against the family. Traditional, biblical values for the home were bombarded by educators, authors and sociologists. Statistics reveal a phenomenal number of homes shattered by divorce, sexual immorality among our younger generation and a rise in the spread of AIDS.

"We are creating a generation of people who live just for the moment, sexually. They really don't know how to build a relationship, control their own desires or how to wait for things," Stafford says. "They will end up with multiple marriages, broken homes, lonely and with all the unfortunate societal baggage that goes along with that. Society will go downhill."

"I still endorse the commitment of the Sexual Revolution and the early women's movement to forging ... new forms of love and friendship— including sexual ones."

Sexual Liberation Should Continue

Judith Levine

Judith Levine is a journalist and critic for *The Village Voice*, a liberal weekly newspaper in New York City. She has also written about sex, feminism, families, and relationships for other magazines. In the following viewpoint, Levine writes that in the age of AIDS and other sexually transmitted diseases, many people are calling for a return to traditional, monogamous sexual values. Levine argues that we should instead continue sexual liberation.

As you read, consider the following questions:

1. According to Levine, how has AIDS affected sexual freedom?
2. What does Levine consider to be the first step toward changing society?
3. What, according to the author, should be done to promote sexual liberation?

Judith Levine, "Thinking About Sex," *Tikkun*, March/April 1988. Reprinted with permission.

In the past decade we've witnessed sex the question transformed into sex the problem. The problem of teenage pregnancy has become the problem of teenage sex, so we try to teach abstinence instead of contraception and convince ourselves that teenagers have sex only because of peer pressure. AIDS is perceived not as a horrible disease of the body, but as the wasting away of the morals of the body politic. The cure is to contain, not the virus, but nonconventional, nonmonogamous sex.

But you don't have to travel far rightward to discover such attitudes. The middle is rife with them, too. . . . No Congress member objects when Jesse Helms fulminates on the Senate floor about "safe sodomy." Bill Moyers speculates that promiscuity—too many undisciplined young cocks strutting around the inner city's roosts—is the cause of the black family's dissolution. Jesse Jackson, instead of refuting him, drops his economic analysis and preaches a return to the church and its sexual morality. On NBC's "Scared Sexless," host Connie Chung reacts quizzically to Education Secretary William Bennett's remark that "AIDS may give us an opportunity to discourage [sex], and that might be a good thing." But she concludes that, plagues or no, less sex is better, especially for teenagers. She doesn't say why.

In response to all this, the left says nothing. In fact, it consistently puts sex at the bottom of the agenda (my mother has been fighting with my father, both of them old leftists, for forty years about the political centrality of abortion) or demonstrates downright antisex and antipleasure biases. In the 1980s, ever more squeamish about appearing unserious, it distances itself from popular culture (which is all about fun) and from prosex feminists, gays, and other erotic minorities for whom sexual freedom is a fundamental struggle. This is more than an abstract problem: according to the Centers for Disease Control, in the 1990s AIDS may kill more Americans annually than were lost during the entire Vietnam War, yet no left group makes the epidemic a forefront issue.

A Revolutionary Goal

Meanwhile, progressives dismiss the Sexual Revolution as a childish flight of caprice, and though they don't see AIDS as the scourge of God, they use the disease as a justification for endorsing certain kinds of sex and relationships and censuring others. Not as coldhearted as Bennett, but equally insulting to the people dying, these "progressives" find in AIDS the silver lining of newly "meaningful," committed sex. Even from the gay community a pious monogamism emanates—*viz* the mass marriage ceremony at the gay and lesbian march on Washington.

As for feminists, a small rowdy band of prosex guerrillas like No More Nice Girls carries the flame of women's sexual freedom, but all around them the flame dims to a flicker. Influential moderates like Betty Friedan eschew public discourses on lesbianism and sex as "exhibitionist," and steer activism elsewhere. In the early 1980s, abortion is suddenly a "family" issue, and a secondary one at that. If there were good daycare and socialized medicine, the argument runs, we'd all want children, and the demand for abortion would disappear. Lately, abortion finds itself nestling under the antiseptic rubric of "reproductive freedom," with forced caesareans, *in vitro* fertilization, surrogacy, and other politics of modern motherhood. It's as if sex—which, if I'm not mistaken, is the cause of pregnancy—had nothing to do with it. . . .

All this distresses me mightily. . . . I consider pleasure a revolutionary goal. And I still endorse the commitment of the Sexual Revolution and the early women's movement to forging new personal alliances, new forms of love and friendship—including sexual ones. Though never a smash-monogamy zealot, I believe in destabilizing traditional sexual setups and struggling, as we did in the 1960s and 1970s, with the emotions that go with such a cultural upheaval.

The Benefits of Sex

Sex is normal human behavior, a powerful drive that we are all born with, as natural as hunger and thirst. It enables us to bring new life into the world, and at the same time it is pleasurable. One cannot deny that we are often first attracted sexually to the one we decide to spend a good deal of time with, even our entire lifetime. Sex, also, is closely tied to our very vitality, our physical and mental vigor, our capacity to grow and create and act.

John Langone, *Like, Love, Lust*, 1980.

At the risk of sounding "nostalgic," or, in the age of AIDS, either frivolous or mad, I contend that we can't change society if we don't challenge the sexual hegemony of the nuclear family and resist its enforcement of adult heterosexual monogamy and its policing of all other forms of sexuality within it and outside it. Supporting "alternative" families or giving lip service to gay rights isn't enough; we must militantly stand up for everybody whose sexuality falls outside "acceptable" bourgeois arrangements—even far outside of them.

But you can't do this without asking fundamental questions about sex. Questions like, is monogamy better? (My answer: not necessarily.) What's wrong with kids having sex ? (Often, nothing.) Why is it worse to pay for sex than to pay for someone to listen to your intimate problems or care for your infant? (You tell me.) You can't ask those questions if you whisk sexuality to the bottom of the list of "serious issues" after peace, or childcare, or even AIDS.

Indeed, AIDS should have us thinking harder than ever about how to preserve pleasure in our lives. If the disease limits our options, at the very least we don't have to be sanctimonious about it! I may currently like having sex with only one person, but I don't like feeling I'd better sleep with him exclusively from now on, or death will us part. Fear of death is about as felicitous a motivation for monogamy as fear of impoverishment is for staying married.

Sex Is Good

We shouldn't be looking for meaning in sex at all, in fact, but rather trying to strip implicit meaning from sex. I don't mean pushing for casual sex, but allowing a separation of sex from commitment and then, by conscious decision only, rejoining the two. This would not only emancipate women to make the choices men have always made about what sex means in a given relationship, it would enhance the possibility for stronger alliances, both passionate and emotional.

In thinking about how that could be done, I recall a 1983 piece by Edmund White, "Paradise Found," about his circle of gay friends and lovers. Outside the rules and expectations of family, relationships were highly fluid. Unlike heterosexual couples, who date, become monogamous, marry, integrate into one another's families, have children, and adjust their sex lives accordingly, a gay lover could be anything from a trick to a husband, or over time, both. Though radical gayness singled out sexuality as an essence of identity, it also freed relationships from being defined by sex. In the novel *Dancing in the Dark*, Janet Hobhouse described "these loving friends, admitted into their Giotto heaven one by one as each 'came out' and professed the faith, free to touch and kiss like angels. . . ." If the meanings of sex were myriad, the use of sex was plain: pleasure.

Our task today is not to pine away in nostalgia, but neither is it to disavow the sexual liberation we fought for in the past decades. We need to keep pleasure as a vital part of the progressive vision at the same time as we confront AIDS, which vanquishes pleasure more powerfully than any repression the right or the left could ever dream up. We must help our children feel that sex is good in an era when sex can bring death, and learn how to relate sexually to each other when new relationships are short-circuited, and old ones sustained, by fear. . . .

Safe Sex Education

Good sex education is safe sex education too. Helping kids to be aware of their bodies—of health and contraception, masturbation, sensual touching, and fantasy as well as intercourse—and of their feelings about sexuality can only make them better able to practice safe and egalitarian sex in what could be history's most honest chapter of sexual relations.

Sexual behavior, moreover, should never be governed by a separate category of morality. If we want our kids to balance their own desires with responsibility and consideration for others, to express their needs and objections freely but cooperate within a community, then we should practice and teach our kids these values in sex, too. Teaching abstinence as "right" is not only puritanical and ineffective in limiting sexual activity, but it fuels prejudice against people whose sexual expression may be more flagrant, and it implies that disease is a punishment for sin.

Too Far To Surrender

Those on the frontier of sexual choice keep alive options which might otherwise be buried under a reactionary avalanche. What seems experimental and marginal at one time may become an important option—for all women—at another time. . . . Women have come too far to surrender the range of possibilities opened up by a sexual revolution.

Barbara Ehrenreich, Elizabeth Hess, and Gloria Jacobs, *Ms.*, July 1986.

AIDS presents one of the biggest challenges in history to our survival as a loving community. Both safety and compassion require us to stop seeing those we've been taught to revile as the Other. When we are ruled by fear and alienation, it is easy for extreme attitudes and repressive policies to start sounding reasonable. On the day of the 1987 gay march in Washington, D.C., for instance, the *New York Post*'s lead story, headlined AIDS MONSTER, stereotyped the classic diseased and depraved homosexual, hunted by police for molesting what seemed like countless boys. It is easy to see through the *Post*'s bigotry, but the story plays on the same assumption that supports mandatory testing and disclosure: that people with AIDS lie, remain selfishly ignorant, and deliberately infect—murder—others, so desperate and devoid of social responsibility are they. When "they" are so unlike "us," Draconian measures like tattooing or quarantine seem necessary "for the greater good." In reality, the greater good demands reaching deep to find our human similarities and also respecting our sexual differences.

The antisex hysteria of the 1980s also presents a great challenge to us as lovers. Fear and malaise are counter-aphrodisiac (the number one complaint sex therapists hear is lack of desire). We need not exacerbate them with self-righteousness. . . .

Just Say Yes

Where can we look for prosex messages in the AIDS era? I found one in the most threatened quarter, the gay community, in the educational comic books once distributed by the Gay Men's Health Crisis. These depicted sexual types from leathermen to clones, gorgeously built and hung every one, having phone sex, masturbating, or role-playing, all with minimum risk and maximum heat. Explicitly, humorously sexual, indeed happily pornographic, these pamphlets were pragmatic: they met their constituency where it lived and did not try to preach living differently. But they implied more—that it's unnecessary to foment aversion to sex through moralizing or hyperbolizing. Death is aversion enough. It's driven many back into the closet and made celibates of countless more.

Instead, the lascivious comic-book hunks are saying: affirm sex. While death is all around us, let us nurture pleasure—for pleasure is life. Even now, especially now, just say yes.

"We've sold ourselves into another form of slavery—a subservience to untamed sensuality."

Sexual Liberation Should End

Paul A. Mickey with William Proctor

Paul A. Mickey is a United Methodist minister who has worked as a marital counselor. William Proctor has written forty books, including many religious works. In the following viewpoint, they write that sexual liberation has destroyed intimacy in relationships, decreased desire, and most seriously of all, spread AIDS. They argue for a return to monogamy.

As you read, consider the following questions:

1. According to Mickey and Proctor, what has been the result of an "excess of sex"?
2. What do the authors believe has been the most alarming cost of promiscuity?
3. What factors do the authors believe will improve sexual relations?

We've torn down many barriers that once restrained us from freewheeling sexual expression. We think we are an "enlightened" people, as comfortable with the practice of coitus, concupiscence, and cohabitation as we are with small talk about the weather or the world situation. Time-honored warnings such as "Thou shalt not commit adultery" or "Fornicators shall not inherit the kingdom of God" are definitely old hat these days, as irrelevant as yesterday's newspaper.

Ironically, though, many find themselves in bondage to the very sexual liberty that once was so boldly proclaimed as the dawning of a new age. In my own counseling practice, I've witnessed sex-related complaints mushroom to disturbing levels during the past decade. And what I'm seeing in my office is but a small mirror, reflecting a much broader problem throughout the nation.

I'm talking about a sexual libertine's lockup we've built for ourselves. This is a prison with a number of formidable walls, the first of which might be called the wall of illegitimacy. The signs of our sex prison are varied and frightening—and often the main victims are the most innocent. For example, nearly 18 percent of all infants born in the United States were born to unwed mothers, according to a U.S. Census Bureau Study released in 1986. Among younger women, those eighteen to twenty-four years of age, the illegitimacy rate was more than 31 percent—a figure that includes 20.2 percent white and 74.5 percent black women. . . .

Building Emotional Walls

On a psychological level, we've created some very serious frustrations for ourselves. The excess of sex hasn't caused us to want it more. Instead, we want it less. In fact, a "lack of desire" has been the prime problem reported with at least half of the patients of members of the American Association of Sex Educators, Counselors, and Therapists.

"We are seeing an increase of people with reduced sex interest," confides Dr. William Masters, the leading light of contemporary sex therapy.

Other evidence confirms that those who have been engaging in unlimited sex may not be enjoying it all that much. One-third of the women surveyed in a *New England Journal of Medicine* study said that they had trouble getting particularly excited during intercourse. Interestingly enough, many husbands were blind to their wives' lack of fulfillment: Only one husband out of seven thought his wife had any problems in bed. To put it bluntly, a significant number of people actually regard all the recent sexual activity as a crashing bore. At least that was the opinion of more than a third of the women and 16 percent of the men surveyed by Dr. Ellen Frank of the University of Pittsburgh. . . .

© 1987 by NEA, Inc   3-B

"I've got it! Let's talk about moral values
and sexual restraint."

Jim Berry. Reprinted by permission of NEA, Inc.

Perhaps the most alarming result of our new sexuality is one
that threatens our health and, indeed, our very lives. We're currently confronted with an epidemic of venereal diseases, including
the deadly AIDS (Acquired Immune Deficiency Syndrome). AIDS
is a disease that mostly afflicts the homosexual community and
intravenous-drug users. But steadily, it's also becoming a major
problem among heterosexuals. Various studies have confirmed that
the AIDS virus can be transmitted to men or women through

34

normal sexual intercourse—though anal and oral sex continue to be the most common modes of sexual infection.

Recently two women who had participated in "swinging" sex clubs in Minnesota were found to carry the AIDS virus. Despite the wide national publicity about AIDS, they and other members of their swingers' club had been mostly unaware of the risks carried by promiscuity.

A Tragic Triangle

AIDS tragedies also may emerge in more traditional settings, far from the exotic, often weird atmosphere that surrounds orgy-oriented sex organizations. Take the tragic case of a Cleveland husband and wife that was reported in a letter to *The New England Journal of Medicine* in 1986. The married man, who was bisexual, got the disease from homosexual one-night stands during his business trips to New York City. He had regular intercourse with his wife before they realized he had AIDS. Even after his case was diagnosed, medical tests conducted on the wife gave her a clean bill of health—at least at first.

Eventually the husband died of AIDS. The wife, thinking she had escaped unscathed, began an affair with her neighbor, a bachelor, a few months later. But unfortunately, later medical tests revealed that the woman *had* been infected with AIDS; the earlier tests on her simply had failed to detect the problem. Within a short period, the woman died of the disease. And now the circle of tragedy is almost complete: Medical tests show that her bachelor lover also has been infected.

When such individual problems are projected to the national and international scene, the outlook is frightening. Experts estimate that five million Americans may carry the AIDS virus by 1991. Not only that, by 1991 the AIDS epidemic may kill Americans at the rate of sixty thousand a year, or more than the number who die now in traffic mishaps. . . .

Breaking Down the Prison

Obviously we've got a problem—a very *big* problem—with sex in our society. We started out believing that the sexual revolution would free us from archaic rules and outmoded traditions that had always shackled intimate relationships. But instead we've sold ourselves into another form of slavery—a subservience to untamed sensuality that alternately bores us, rips our intimate relationships to shreds, and even threatens to maim or kill us in frightening numbers.

But still there is hope. Sex doesn't have to be your slavemaster; it doesn't have to be a prison. In fact, the right kind of sex can be a wonderful, intoxicating thing! To put this another way, many of the romantic stories and love poems you've read are rooted in the truth about sex as it was originally intended to be. When

Robert Burns wrote, "O, my luve is like a red, red rose," he wasn't just engaging in fantasy! "True love," of the type that Bing Crosby extolled when he crooned the song by that name, is actually a possibility!

When you begin a romantic relationship—and are careful to fit sexual expressions in their proper place—you can expect the exhiliration and tenderness of that fabled first love to continue. Even as you and your lover lose some of the bloom of first romance and as the initial flames of passion burn down to steady, warm embers of deep affection there's no reason why you can't get a thrill out of holding hands, snuggling up on the sofa—and enjoying a bit of high excitement in the bedroom.

"*The best defense against contracting AIDS . . . is sexual abstinence before marriage and sexual faithfulness within marriage—for* both *partners.*"

AIDS Proves Sexual Liberation Is Harmful

Donald D. Schroeder

AIDS has made many people reevaluate the sexual revolution. In the following viewpoint, Donald D. Schroeder, a senior writer for the religious monthly *The Plain Truth*, argues that AIDS is a sign that the sexual revolution was dangerous. The spread of AIDS, he contends, can be stopped only by repudiating casual sex.

As you read, consider the following questions:

1. What makes AIDS unique among sexually transmitted diseases, according to the author?
2. According to Schroeder, why hasn't AIDS affected the sexual revolution?
3. Why are condoms not a solution to avoiding AIDS, according to the author?

Donald D. Schroeder, "The Moral Message Behind STDs," *The Plain Truth*, February 1988. Copyright © 1988 Worldwide Church of God. All rights reserved.

Nothing in recent decades has jarred free-swinging sexual attitudes and life-styles—and will continue to do so—more than incurable sexually transmissible diseases.

Age-old venereal diseases such as syphilis and gonorrhea didn't faze many having a sexual fling. There was some drug available to cure them.

But during the '70s a new kind of venereal disease, genital herpes, suddenly exploded into a full-fledged epidemic that swiftly cut through the ranks. No drug could cure this recurring, painful and socially upsetting disease. But while herpes made many persons more cautious, symptoms were treatable and it was rarely fatal.

Then in the early 1980s, health officials were startled to discover that an unrecognized bacterium called chlamydia was causing perhaps two or three times as many cases of female pelvic inflammations than gonorrhea, and as much or more sterility. Penicillin wouldn't stop this pathogen. Other stronger and more costly antibiotics were needed.

A First in History

During this same period, health officials were confounded when a new virus-caused disease—later named Acquired Immune Deficiency Syndrome (AIDS)—burst out of obscurity among male homosexuals and intravenous drug abusers. Never before had humanity experienced a sexually transmissible disease that destroys the infected person's immune system, leaving it powerless against many other infections and diseases.

For the first time in modern history, humanity is faced with an incurable, sexually transmissible disease that apparently has a 100 percent fatality rate once serious symptoms develop. Just since 1981, within seven years' time of the first reportings, this fatal disease has spread virtually worldwide.

So rampantly and quickly has AIDS spread in some populations that health officials are telling us that *every* sexually active person—that is, every person who engages in extramarital, homosexual or bisexual sex activity—along with sexual partners, and *every* drug abuser (and their sexual partners) who shares needles or receives improperly sterilized medical injections is *potentially at risk* of AIDS.

Unlike many other sexually transmitted pathogens, Human Immunodeficiency Virus—the AIDS virus—is a complex and changing virus. The fact that a safe preventative vaccine may not be available before the mid-'90s, if ever, has had an effect on sexual activity. Others have seen treatment for the terrible ravages of AIDS often pauperize its victims.

While AIDS captures world attention at the moment, health officials are worried about new epidemics of sexually transmissible pathogens that will infect many future sexual experimenters.

One little-known pathogenic virus that gynecologists and cancer specialists are voicing alarm about is a growing epidemic of genital warts caused by the human papilloma virus. The genital variety of papilloma virus is mostly spread sexually and has a strong link with cervical cancer.

"It's become epidemic," says Dr. Palmer C. Evans, a Tucson, Arizona, obstetrician and gynecologist. "The reason why is that the sexual revolution of the '60s has set us up for what's happening now. . . . The sexually transmitted viruses are the fruits of that sexual revolution, and we are reaping them now."

Earl Engleman. Reprinted with permission.

Like genital herpes and the AIDS virus, a victim infected with human papilloma virus is infected for life, though genital warts can be removed and symptoms treated. If genital warts get out of control, they can cause disfigurement of infected areas, obstruction of urinary or defecatory processes, or irritation and secondary infections.

New Dangers

Another pathogen that will cause alarm to sexually active persons in the future is already a big worry to health officials. It is super strains of gonorrhea that are now resisting all but the most powerful and expensive of antibiotics. Gonorrhea has historically eventually become resistant to every drug used against it.

"We are beginning to run out of drugs," warns Dr. John W. Boslego of Walter Reed Army Institute of Research in Washington, D.C. We are rapidly approaching the years when the medical profession could end up with no drugs able to fight certain strains of this ancient crippler and sterilizer.

Meanwhile, other researchers warn of the possibility that there are unrecognized pathogens—especially viruses—that could form the basis of new epidemics. Such pathogens spread epidemically in sexually active groups.

The grave danger with many of these diseases is most infected persons do not know they are infected. Millions do not yet show symptoms of AIDS and other dangerous sexually transmissible diseases but yet are capable of infecting others.

But if you think the threat of serious diseases is so scary that the permissiveness of the Sexual Revolution is over, as some authorities state, you are mistaken.

Human nature is such that many individuals who do not strongly adhere to high sexual standards of mutually faithful, monogamous marital sexual relations often willingly blind their mind to dangers of these diseases and other serious consequences.

Long ago, the Creator revealed to man that sexual relations are to be confined to marriage to protect the family unit and bless all society. Premarital, homosexual and other extramarital sex acts are forbidden in numerous instructions of Scripture. Millions, however, have rejected the Creator's revealed instructions.

The disturbing fact is, despite the frightening aspects of incurable, sexually transmissible diseases, uncounted millions still take risks and plunge into promiscuous sex to fulfill their own selfish desires and lusts. They rationalize they are at little or no risk, or they simply don't care.

Studies indicate that between 25 percent and 40 percent of married women, and around 50 percent of married men in the United States allow themselves to engage in one or more extramarital affairs during their married life.

And according to U.S. Department of Health and Human Services data, more than 70 percent of U.S. teenagers have sexual relations before age 20. Only 15 percent of teens in a survey reported changing their sexual behavior because of fear of AIDS. Homosexual males in areas where AIDS risk is considered relatively low are either refusing to believe they are at risk or are shrugging off precautions fatalistically. It is only a matter of time before such areas will experience their own epidemic of AIDS.

Questioning Sexual Liberation

The AIDS crisis has crystallized ruminations that had already begun to take shape. . . . It makes even more urgent the work of those in the homosexual community who promulgate an ethic of responsibility and care instead of promiscuity; and it prompts heterosexuals to rethink whether the sexual liberation standard was from its inception the generalization of a norm of adolescent male sexuality writ large onto the wider social fabric.

Jean Bethke Elshtain, *Tikkun*, March/April 1988.

Even though condoms have been, somewhat inaccurately, equated with "safe sex," only about half of those who have multiple sexual partners said they had bought condoms at least once within the last year.

Millions are unaware that condoms, while they reduce chances of producing pregnancy, are still quite chancy in preventing many sexually transmissible diseases, especially viral ones. Condoms break or fail about 10 percent or more of the time. In addition, many persons buying them do not use them.

Risky Business

Now with increasing emphasis by health officials and the media that heterosexuals in the United States and other developed nations have an AIDS risk significantly lower than homosexuals and intravenous drug abusers, you can expect many promiscuously minded heterosexuals to drop their guard even more and continue their risky life-style.

Historically, great numbers of sexually active persons take chances despite disease dangers to their own and others' lives to fulfill their erotic lusts. And since it often takes five to ten years for an AIDS infection to develop into the disease, and other venereal infections often do not show early symptoms, you will find many such persons denying they are at high risk, when they are at risk or even infected.

Within society are great cross-currents of values. Millions are bereft of any purpose in life but that of fulfilling their own desires and pleasures. Many respect no authority or values but their own. The Bible describes such "perilous times."

"If it feels good, do it," was commonly preached in the '60s, '70s and early '80s. Now, as we approach the end of the '80s and go into the 1990s, such thinking could kill you.

Will you be among the millions who will not face up to the staggering dangers of AIDS and more than 20 other serious sexually transmissible diseases until it is too late? You must if you care about your future and loved ones. The moral message of STDs and AIDS is *SCREAMING* at us!

Medical science has, belatedly, been forced to agree with what sexual morality has taught for thousands of years. The best defense against contracting AIDS and most serious sexually transmissible diseases is sexual abstinence before marriage and sexual faithfulness within marriage—for *both* partners.

Many scoff at such morality. But it's no longer a scoffing matter if you want to protect your own life and that of your mate, or future mate, and children.

"I'm also determined not to allow all this hysteria . . . to box me into believing I can't have sex again till I've picked my white-bread mate for life."

AIDS Should Not Be Used To End Sexual Liberation

Katie Monagle

Sexual freedom should be an option even in the age of AIDS, according to Katie Monagle, the author of the following viewpoint. A writer for the feminist monthly magazine, *Ms.*, Monagle believes people should respond to AIDS by adopting safe sex practices, not by abstaining from sex. She argues that AIDS is being used as an excuse to smother sexuality.

As you read, consider the following questions:

1. Why does Monagle feel threatened by the new morality?
2. What does Monagle suggest to stop the spread of AIDS?
3. According to the author, what will be accomplished by rejecting the new morality?

Katie Monagle, "Nice Girls Do," *Ms.*, May 1989. Reprinted with permission of *Ms.* Magazine.

The "new morality" is giving me a bad case of déjà vu, even though I'm only 23. This time the danger of AIDS is the rationale for sticking to "old-fashioned" values that create a sexual double standard and legitimate only heterosexual relationships with people of one's same race and class. However, I got these same messages during my childhood and teen years—only then there wasn't a convenient disease to mask the sexual politics. Then, the reasons for holding people, especially women, in check were based on ideas of class and respectability, religion, racism, and homophobia.

When I began my official journey into sexuality with my first real kiss at 14, I had few inhibitions other than keeping my hymen intact until I was at least in love, if not married. I was attending an all-girl, nun-run Catholic high school. When I got to see boys, what registered was the tingly possibility of a fooling-around kind of fun, and the more pragmatic goal of being socially acceptable: there was obviously something wrong about a girl without a beau.

Kissing and making out were the most fun I'd ever had. I lost my library card, forsook *The Love Boat* and *Fantasy Island*, and concentrated on the telephone and my social life. I knew my precoital sexual activity needed to be kept from my parents. They had always told me, and I knew they were sincere, that sex inside marriage is beautiful. Until I was 14, I believed them.

Sex Inside Love

Later, I reinterpreted their message to fit my life: sex inside *love* is beautiful. I figured that until love knocked at my heart, anything but the actual deed could be done. To me, as to many teenagers, my parents weren't the most reliable judges of right and wrong— my peers were, and I still remember when I got the message from them that I was doing something wrong.

The day after a newly acquired "best" friend and I had double-dated, she teased me—amid a group of her old and my new friends—about how she and her date had laughed at the way my date and I shook the car with our enthusiastic "making out." Those few minutes of my life in the sunny courtyard of an old New Orleans convent and girls' school linger sharply in my memory nine years later. Instead of titters and mutual girlish confidences, my new friends looked uncomfortable, and eyed me appraisingly. I felt gross, as though—despite my "virginity"—I belonged to the ranks of the sleazy, easy girls.

Now these narrow-minded values I've spent almost half my life trying to escape are the cornerstone of "the biggest social movement since the sixties" (this information is courtesy of *Good Housekeeping*'s New Traditionalist ad campaign). Young people are more conservative now than a generation ago, we're told. Casual sex is out. Heterosexuality and monogamy are in, lauded as the only ways to have Safe Sex and Beautiful Relationships.

I feel threatened by the New Morality. It's not just sex that's under attack—it's my ability to be me, whoever I am, without being subjected to painful censure in my personal or professional life. I'm seeing not just more conventional relationships among my peers, but also a license to censure other people's decisions about how to run their sex and their lives. Although my friends in the urban Northeast are politically liberal, socially permissive, and not particularly monogamy-minded, I'm afraid I won't be very comfortable outside our circle.

Pressure and Prejudice

Whether due to the old morality or the new, the pressure is on to be monogamous—single or married. Jane, a 23-year-old New York woman pursuing a promising career in finance, believes, "People would think I was crazy if I just slept with someone— even if they weren't thinking in terms of AIDS." Liz, 24, an old friend who lives with her boyfriend in Queens, New York, senses condescension and pity for women who are not married or almost-married—especially from women who sowed their oats during freer days and now have naturally evolved into monogamy. "The glamour of being single is gone," Liz says.

Greater Heights

AIDS and the other less serious contaminants of eros do not have to spell the end of renegade sexuality, despite what the self-proclaimed guardians of our moral health excitedly declaim. On the contrary, I believe these new dangers of the flesh impel us to even greater heights of sexual imagination.

David Talbot, *Utne Reader*, June/July 1986.

And it's not only our sex lives that Liz sees endangered by the New Morality. "I think AIDS will just make people more prejudiced than they already are—make them think it was wrong and foolish to have been liberal in any way. There are all these people out there who aren't prejudiced against blacks or homosexuals in the stereotypical sense—don't use nasty labels—but who feel that AIDS is a 'minority problem.' People are being prejudiced in a covert way."

Mark, who is 25, a Wall Street attorney, and gay, says that in the gay community the emphasis is not on how much sex one has, but on taking precautions and communicating honestly about one's sexual and drug use history. Still, "People think I should cut down on the number of my sex partners rather than making sure

I'm totally safe. Deep down, everyone wants to find one person to fall in love with, but in the meantime they would have casual sex. Now 'in the meantime' is gone."

But the double standard that always went along with monogamy —setting limits on women and gays but leaving promiscuous heterosexual men uncensored—is still with us. Brian, a 24-year-old San Franciscan still prowling on the singles scene, has been the lover of almost 40 women in his short lifetime. Yet he sheepishly admits to living by the double standard: "If I have sex with someone, afterward I shouldn't have to feel like, 'Wow, I don't like this person anymore' because she's had sex with me. But sometimes I do feel that, if it's a one-night stand."

Condom Sense

Of women who carry condoms in their purses, Brian says, "I think maybe these girls sleep around a lot and that's why they're carrying these condoms." He explains that "all guys are sluts," but "when I say 'male slut' I kind of think positively. A male slut is a guy who is good with the girls, a guy who can pick up women." About female "sluts," though, Brian thinks "negatively. That's terrible, but it's true."

Yet Brian—he who doesn't like women who carry condoms— will now, because of AIDS, "always wear a condom. I used to claim I couldn't get a hard-on if I wore a rubber," he confesses. "That was my big philosophy. When I was having sex, it was like, 'Grunt, I hope you have, grunt, grunt, something. No? Okay, we'll chance it.' Now I'll use a condom. It's important. I don't want to die for it."

I used to have problems asking men to wear condoms. They'd say no, or whine and prophesy that it just "wouldn't work." I'd get embarrassed by the fact that I could produce a condom when they couldn't—it made me look so eager. Finally I got tired of the conflict with the men and myself, and blew off even suggesting prophylactic protection for a while. Hell, we lily-white and middle class aren't really in danger anyway. Right?

For that, I suffered. I suffered a minor medical problem. I suffered a blow to my personal pride: never have my feminist politics been more pertinent to my real life, and I failed myself. And my partner.

Still Having Fun

Well, I don't have a problem anymore. I want sex, I want my life, and I want to live my life with a sense of pride in myself— which means doing what I know is responsible and right, even if it makes me uncomfortable sometimes. Besides, I didn't like the fact that a little bit of sexism intimidated me enough to suppress my principles and endanger people's lives.

However, I do think AIDS is being used as an excuse for moving back into the old 1950s-style morality. I am aware of AIDS and, despite the old adage "Never say never," I will never have sex without protection before my partner and I have carefully examined each other's doctor's certificates. But I'm also determined not to allow all this hysteria and conservative social coercion to box me into believing I can't have sex again till I've picked my white-bread mate for life. Monogamy, bigotry, and homophobia won't save me from the hazards of modern life.

There have been a lot of places in my life where I didn't feel free to be me—it wasn't cool, respectable, or attractive. I wasn't happy in those places because I couldn't be part of a community. Sometimes I'm not brave enough to be different in a seemingly united world. So I don't want caution to turn into rights-reducing fanaticism that makes all sorts of people into outsiders. We still have some degrees of freedom, medically and socially, about what we do in bed, with whom, and why. I want that freedom for myself, and I endorse it for others. And I still wanna have fun.

a critical thinking activity

Distinguishing Between Fact and Opinion

This activity is designed to help develop the basic reading and thinking skill of distinguishing between fact and opinion. Consider the following statement: "AIDS cases were first reported in 1981." This is a factual statement because it could be proven by checking with the Centers for Disease Control, a government health research agency which maintains statistics on the epidemic. But the statement, "The promiscuity of the sexual revolution was the sole cause of AIDS," is an opinion. The cause of AIDS is a highly debated issue on which many people would disagree.

When investigating controversial issues it is important that one be able to distinguish between statements of fact and statements of opinion. It is also important to recognize that not all statements of fact are true. They may appear to be true, but some are based on inaccurate or false information. For this activity, however, we are concerned with understanding the difference between those statements which appear to be factual and those which appear to be based primarily on opinion.

Most of the following statements are taken from the viewpoints in this chapter. Consider each statement carefully. *Mark O for any statement you believe is an opinion or interpretation of facts. Mark F for any statement you believe is a fact. Mark I for any statement you believe is impossible to judge.*

If you are doing this activity as a member of a class or group, compare your answers with those of other class or group members. Be able to defend your answers. You may discover that others come to different conclusions than you. Listening to the reasons others present for their answers may give you valuable insights in distinguishing between fact and opinion.

O = *opinion*
F = *fact*
I = *impossible to judge*

48

1. Sex is a tired substitute for love.

2. The number of syphilis cases is creeping up after a five-year decline.

3. A survey of 12,000 single men and women showed a decline in the approval of premarital sex.

4. There is nothing wrong with children having sex.

5. Only women who sleep around a lot carry condoms.

6. AIDS is a disease that mostly affects the homosexual community and intravenous drug users.

7. For two-career couples, especially those with children, sex is only for special occasions.

8. Sex is boring, according to more than one-third of the women and sixteen percent of the men surveyed recently.

9. Deep down, everyone wants to find one person to fall in love with.

10. AIDS causes great suffering and often reduces its victims to poverty.

11. One gay and lesbian march on Washington featured a mass marriage ceremony.

12. If people lived by the Bible, sexually transmitted diseases like AIDS would not be a threat.

13. In the 1990s AIDS may kill more Americans annually than were lost during the entire Vietnam War.

14. We are rapidly approaching the time when the medical profession will have no drugs to fight gonorrhea.

15. We can't change society if we don't challenge the nuclear family and resist its enforcement of adult heterosexual monogamy.

16. Young people today don't know how to build a relationship or control their own desires.

17. Conservatives are advising a return to traditional morality to halt the spread of AIDS.

18. Homosexual practices helped spread AIDS.

19. The sexual revolution involved the rejection of traditional morality.

Periodical Bibliography

The following articles have been selected to supplement the diverse views presented in this chapter.

James J. Bennet	"The Data Game," *The New Republic*, February 13, 1989.
Anne Husted Burleigh	"Why Fidelity?" *Crisis*, March 1989.
Jack Douglas	"The Sexual Modernists," *The Family in America*, May 1987. Available from the Rockford Institute Center, PO Box 416, Mount Morris, IL 60154.
Sol Gordon and Rob Tielman	"Is the Sexual Revolution Over?" *Free Inquiry*, Fall 1987. Available from the Council for Democratic and Secular Humanism, 3159 Bailey Ave., Buffalo, NY 14215.
Simi Horwitz	"Sex Is Alive & Well," *Harper's Bazaar*, November 1988.
D.F. Kinlaw	"Short-Order Sexuality," *Christianity Today*, February 20, 1987.
Julia Kristeva	"AIDS and Eros," *Harper's Magazine*, October 1987.
William H. Masters et al.	"Sex in the Age of AIDS," *Newsweek*, March 14, 1988.
Donald D. Schroeder	"Sex: The Big Risk?" *The Plain Truth*, April 1989. Available from *The Plain Truth*, 300 W. Green St., Pasadena, CA 91123.
Ian Shoales	"Sex Is Over," *Mademoiselle*, August 1987.
Tim Stafford	"Great Sex: Reclaiming a Christian Sexual Ethic," *Christianity Today*, October 2, 1987.
Robert Staples	"The Sexual Revolution and the Black Middle Class," *Ebony*, August 1987.
Judith Stone	"The Sexual Revolution Is Over," *Glamour*, July 1988.
Utne Reader	"Remember Sex?" September/October 1988.
John W. Wauck	"Whatever Happened to Sex?" *The Human Life Review*, Summer 1988. Available from the Human Life Foundation, Inc., 150 E. 35th St., New York, NY 10016.

How Should Society Treat Homosexuality?

SEXUAL VALUES

Chapter Preface

Science has long debated the question of whether homosexuality is a natural condition or a psychological disorder.

For many years it was considered a disorder. But in 1973, the American Psychiatric Association reversed its long-held position on homosexuality. It declared that homosexuality is biologically predetermined and is not a disorder that can be cured. Many who heralded the decision believe society must accept homosexuality and forbid discrimination against gays.

Not everyone agrees with this view, however. Sociologist Edward M. Levine contends that homosexuality is learned. He argues that people who are homosexual were raised in homes where gender roles were confused. Levine and those who agree with him conclude that rather than accept homosexuality, society must reject it. Gays should be pressured to seek psychiatric help so they can become healthy, normal heterosexuals.

Despite all the studies on homosexuality, the question of how society should treat gays continues to inspire debate. The following chapter presents several views relevant to this debate.

"Homosexuality . . . is a healthy, natural, and affirming form of human sexuality for some people."

Homosexuality Is Natural

John Shelby Spong

John Shelby Spong is an Episcopalian bishop who generated much controversy in the Church because of his book, *Living in Sin?* In the following viewpoint, excerpted from this book, Spong argues that homosexuality is a natural sexual preference that should be accepted.

As you read, consider the following questions:

1. What evidence does Spong offer to prove that homosexuality is normal?
2. According to the author, how does society's rejection of homosexuality affect the homosexual?
3. What does Spong hope will be the attitude toward homosexuality in the future?

Contemporary research is today uncovering new facts that are producing a rising conviction that homosexuality, far from being a sickness, sin, perversion, or unnatural act, is a healthy, natural, and affirming form of human sexuality for some people. This research is still in its infancy, relatively speaking, but it has demonstrated a capacity to confront and challenge sexual fear and prejudice that has become entrenched by centuries of repetition. Only in the last few decades have we begun to understand such things as the structure and various functions of the brain, to say nothing of the importance of chromosomes. Discoveries in these areas have had a dramatic effect on our knowledge of human behavior. Specifically, research consistently seems to support the assertion that sexual orientation is not a matter of choice; that it is not related to any environmental influence; that it is not the result of an overbearing mother or an effeminate or absent father or a seductive sexual encounter. Some researchers are finding that certain biochemical events during prenatal life may determine adult sexual orientation, and that once set it is not amenable to change. Though new data are being gathered almost daily, few people working in the area of brain research expect these conclusions to be overturned.

Despite centuries of belief to the contrary, it is slowly dawning on us that the seat of sexual arousal is the brain, not the genitalia. To put it bluntly, this means that the brain is the primary sex organ of the body. A person's sexual orientation and what he or she finds sexually exciting are functions of that person's brain. An understanding of these new findings in the field of human sexuality must therefore begin with a look at modern discoveries about neurophysiology and its role in human learning.

Examples from Nature

In the animal world the line between male and female is not as rigid as many sex-role ideologues would have us believe. A report on issues concerning homosexuality produced by the Lutheran Church in America in 1986 cited some fascinating biological studies documenting this:

> Among some species of fish, particularly the coral reef fish, a virtual sex change will occur in order to ensure reproduction. If a male is suddenly removed from his female partners, the most aggressive female first acts as the male, then functions as the male, and eventually even produces sperm. Among guinea pigs, the total repertoire of sexual behavior occurs at that moment when the adult female presents herself to the male for mounting and ejaculation. This experience is changed dramatically when the pregnant female guinea pig is treated with androgens or androgen blockers. In the case of the former, when the female offspring reaches maturity, she mounts other females; in the latter

case, the male offspring presents himself for mounting to other males. Apart from this reversal, no other behavior inappropriate to gender was observed.

These data would seem to indicate that sexual orientation and the behavior that arises from that orientation has a neurobiological explanation.

This conclusion has been further enforced by experimentation on rhesus monkeys. Tests reveal that when testosterone is blocked from male fetuses in utero, it produces behavior in the male offspring traditionally associated with the female monkey. This, despite the fact that no abnormal hormone balance registers after birth, nor does any subsequent hormone treatment change the monkey's activities to behavior more appropriate to the male of the species. These experiments suggest that a chemical process sets the nature of an unalterable sexual response in the brain during gestation. Or, to be quite specific, the "sexing of the brain" is a prenatal occurrence over which neither the fetus nor the parent has any control whatsoever.

In the Natural World

The claim that homosexual acts are unnatural is based on the belief that homosexuals "are going astray from the foundation of the creation." This claim, however, is not supported by evidence from the natural world. Biologists have conclusively demonstrated that homosexual liaisons are not unusual among mammals.

Bradley Shavit Artson, *Tikkun*, February 1988.

These conclusions have been further augmented by the work of Gunter Dörner, director of the Institute of Experimental Endocrinology at the University of Humboldt in East Berlin. When the scientific community began to understand that it was the hypothalamus, located beneath the thalamus in the brain, that controlled the output of the hormones, Dörner set out to find in the hypothalamus of rats what he took to be different male and female sex centers. His experiments revealed that if rats did not get enough of their appropriate sex hormone during development these sex centers would be formed differently, creating in males the sexual behavior of females and vice versa.

Studies of Human Homosexuals

From these data Dörner argued that sexual orientation in a human fetus is also the result of a neurochemical hormone process that occurs in the womb. Male and female homosexuality, he contended, are caused by the prenatal effect on the brain of varying amounts of a main male sex hormone, testosterone. The relative quantity of testosterone available during critical periods of fetal brain development stamps the yet to be born infant with a masculine or feminine orientation, usually but not always in accordance with the genetic sex of the fetus. This is true, he argued, not just in human beings but in monkeys, rats, guinea pigs, birds, and practically everywhere in nature. It remains a fact that among higher mammals homosexuality is found in roughly the same statistical percentages as is found among *Homo sapiens*.

Dörner performed a series of experiments to test his hypothesis. Male rats were deprived of testosterone during the critical fetal period of sexual differentiation in the brain. As predicted, this process produced homosexual behaviors in the adult male rats. Encouraged by this result, he went a step further. Dörner reasoned that if these rats possessed feminized brains, injection with estrogen would produce from the brain a surge of the ovulation hormone known as luteinizing hormone (LH), as if in response to a signal from a nonexistent ovary. When this test was carried out, the predicted response occurred. The same test was then performed on male homosexual human beings, with identical results. The brains of the homosexual males in this experiment responded to the estrogen injection with an LH hormone surge, while the brains of a control group of heterosexual males did not. Dörner believed this demonstrated that the brains of male homosexuals had been, in fact, feminized prior to birth, and that homosexuality is thus physiologically determined by biochemical variables. If true, this finding constitutes a powerful step forward in demonstrating the source and explanation for the reality of homosexuality. . . .

These accounts individually and collectively support the scientific claim that sexual orientation is, in all probability, a matter of the prenatal "sexing of the brain"; that homosexuality is thus a given fact in the nature of a significant portion of people; and that it is unchangeable once set. It is not genetic in nature, therefore it cannot be "bred out" of the species. The only argument remaining is whether or not this represents a malfunction in the natural process of fetal development or is instead a normal variation serving a purpose in the evolutionary process that has not yet been identified. However, any process of nature that occurs one time out of every ten can hardly be called a malfunction. Nature is far too exact, I believe, to admit that level of mistake. We are driven to the realization that what we have long viewed as a moral issue is in fact an ontological issue. Homosexuality is an issue of being itself. . . .

Avoiding Moral Absolutes

Since the evidence points to the conclusion that homosexual persons do not choose their sexual orientation, cannot change it, and constitute a quite normal but minority expression of human sexuality, it is clear that heterosexual prejudice against homosexuals must take its place alongside witchcraft, slavery, and other ignorant beliefs and oppressive institutions that we have abandoned.

Some people fear that accepting this stance will mean that critical judgment must be suspended from all forms of homosexual behavior. That, too, is an irrational manifestation of prejudice. All forms of heterosexual behavior do not receive approval just because we affirm the goodness of heterosexuality. Any sexual behavior can be destructive, exploitative, predatory, or promiscuous, and therefore evil, regardless of the sexes of the parties involved. Whenever any of those conditions exist, a word of moral judgment needs to be spoken. The difficulty comes when a society evaluates heterosexuality per se as good and homosexuality per se as evil. Such moral absolutes eventuate in preferential ethical treatment for heterosexuals: Distinctions will be made for heterosexual people between life-giving and life-destroying behavior, while any and all patterns of sexual behavior arising from a homosexual orientation are condemned as sinful. Such a moral position leaves gay and lesbian persons with no options save denial or suppression. Indeed, many an ecclesiastical body has suggested that these are in fact the only moral choices open to homosexually oriented people. Perhaps we need to be reminded that large numbers of heterosexual people engage in promiscuity, prostitution, rape, child molestation, incest, and every conceivable form of sadomasochism. Further, by refusing to accept any homosexual behavior as normal, this homophobic society drives many gay and lesbian people into the very behavior patterns that the straight world most fears and condemns. . . .

A Part of the Spectrum

I am convinced, personally, that homosexuality is the result of brain formation in utero, that it is not abnormal, that it is a normal part of the spectrum of human sexuality. It is abnormal only in the sense that it is not the norm for the majority; left-handedness is abnormal in the same sense.

John Shelby Spong, *The Advocate*, August 2, 1988.

In time a new understanding of the origin of homosexuality will cause us to lose the irrational anxiety that our children might be seduced into a homosexual lifestyle by some chance encounter. Witch hunts aimed at removing "those people" from positions where they might be quite influential in the lives of our children will be revealed for what they are and will cease. No longer will our own anxiety overwhelm us when we have a fantasy or dream that we fear might be an expression of latent homosexuality. No longer will men have to hide their softer, yielding sides and women their athletic competence, in order to make sure no one suspects them of an evil orientation.

The next stage is being entered when we begin to regard both the homosexual orientation and the heterosexual orientation in and of themselves as neither good nor evil, but only as real and true. Both aspects of human sexuality will ultimately be seen as natural. The recognition is growing that there is a majority orientation and a minority orientation and that both have roles in the enrichment of human life. This change will take time, for ignorance and fear are both tenacious, and prejudice covers human irrationality, making it difficult and frightening to relinquish.

---

*"Homosexuality is psychopathological . . .
heterosexuality alone is healthy."*

Homosexuality Is Unnatural

Edward M. Levine

Edward M. Levine was a sociology professor at Loyola University
in Chicago, Illinois. In the following viewpoint, Levine contends
that scientists have shown that heterosexuality is genetically
programmed into the fetus before birth. Thus, he argues that
homosexuality is an unnatural disorder.

As you read, consider the following questions:

1. According to the author, why do homosexuals wish to
   destroy the family?
2. How do homosexual men harm unmarried women,
   according to Levine?
3. What is the author's opinion of sexual pleasure outside of
   marriage?

Edward M. Levine, "Homosexuality and the Family," *Chronicles*, July 1988. Reprinted
with permission.

For nearly two decades, homosexuals and their sympathizers have increased their efforts to persuade opinion leaders, educators, clergy, government officials, and the public that their sexual lives, though different, are as normal and natural as the heterosexuals'. Since some heterosexuals also engage in sodomy, the homosexuals have claimed that it is only their same-sex orientation that sets them apart from heterosexuals. Regarding this as inconsequential, homosexuals go on to insist that a pluralist society should extend them minority group acceptance and status. In sum, they call for full social approval of their sexual identity and behavior.

Many of those who are familiar with these views consider it a mark of enlightenment and civility to accept them *prima facie*. They do so largely because homosexuals have led them to believe that homosexuality is an "orientation" or "preference" (choice) and is, therefore, as legitimate as any other.

It is well-known, however, that boys of elementary and high school age who are incipient homosexuals are typically subjected to the punishing taunts, derision, and ridicule of their peers. Both common sense and sociological role theory suggest that the desire of such youngsters (and adults) to avoid the rejection and enjoy the acceptance of their peers would alone induce them to spurn homosexuality, if it were really a matter of sexual preference.

Heterosexuality Is Normal

In an unusually informative 1972 article little known outside the psychiatric community, Warren Gadpaille synthesized empirical studies of physiologists whose findings unequivocally show that human heterosexuality is established, in biologically normal individuals (including homosexuals), between the sixth and 12th weeks of fetal life. Hence, all biologically normal males and females are heterosexual at birth.

Other well-established evidence furnished by Bieber, Charles W. Socarides, Stoller, Ovesey, *et al.* indicates that homosexuality results from an overpowering unconscious fear of heterosexuality, generally caused by a domineering mother and a passive-submissive, emotionally absent father (or the other way around).

The significance of these findings is that homosexuality is a psychopathological symptom that can be (and has been) cured in therapy—providing the individual wants to change (which most homosexuals do not). Even more important is that homosexuality can be prevented by parenting that fosters children's innate biopsychological heterosexuality.

Yet, the thrust of the homosexual movement is to deny that homosexuality is psychopathological, that heterosexuality alone is healthy, and that sound parenting is essential to heterosexual gender-identity in adulthood. The logic of homosexuals' claim to normality leads them to reject the importance of marriage and family, of competent child-rearing, and of the moral values that serve as their foundation.

In 1973, yielding to great pressure from homosexual organizations and ideologues, the American Psychiatric Assocation (APA) initiated the change in its official diagnosis of homosexuality as psychopathology. The new policy declared homosexuality psychopathological only for those individuals who sought psychiatric treatment for it. The APA's policy change was followed, two years later, by the American Psychological Association. Both official views are still held up by homosexuals as definitive proof that homosexuality is psychologically and otherwise as healthy as heterosexuality.

These diagnostic redefinitions of homosexuality by leading professional associations have had an adverse impact that extends far beyond the views of therapists, homosexuals, and sexologists. Parents, for example, may be confused about how to rear their children if their values and intuition conflict with the official conclusions of the new priesthood. And their uncertainty will be sensed by their offspring who need parental support for their developing masculinity and femininity.

A Perversion of Nature

There is no natural homosexuality, for homosexuality is precisely a perversion of nature (understood as God's design for human relations). Homosexuals are made, not born; their disorder is developed contrary to their God-given identity, learned in opposition to the created order.

The Arthur S. DeMoss Foundation, *The Rebirth of America*, 1986.

Parents who are indifferent about their children's gender-identity may very well place them at risk of becoming homosexuals, bisexuals, or transsexuals. Rather than admiring and reinforcing their sons' and daughters' sexual differences, some parents studiously adhere to the social fiction of androgyny as a biological fact. For their children, serious heterosexual dysfunctions are possible outcomes of being raised according to this contemporary mythology.

Impersonal Sex

While a good deal has been written about the homosexuals' sexual behavior that sets them apart from society, homosexuals rarely discuss this publicly. Their desire for respectability masks their obsession with sexual gratification as such, regardless of the degradation of both their and their sex partners' individuality. By their own accounts, they endlessly engage in furtive, promiscuous, and impersonal sex with utter strangers in public men's rooms, parks, bathhouses, and elsewhere. Some have reported having as many as 10 different sex partners during an evening, and in 1978 Bell and T.S. Weinberg found that 43 percent of the homosexuals in their study had more than 500 different sex partners in a lifetime.

As for homosexual couples, it is well-known and acknowledged among them that infidelity is their norm. Peter Fisher has candidly written that homosexual "love" is no longer expected to hinge on fidelity. As we are now aware, it is their sexual promiscuity that is largely responsible for the high rate of venereal and other diseases among homosexuals, as well as for the AIDS epidemic that has struck them and, through bisexuals, threatens the rest of us.

In the name of their right to indulge themselves in depersonalized sex, homosexuals have mounted a strong attack on the family as an indispensable institution. In 1971, for example, Dennis Altman, a leading and articulate homosexual spokesman, envisaged sexual liberation as putting an end to monogamy and "the nuclear family as the central organizing principle of society." Altman believes in communal child-rearing that would involve nonparent adults, including homosexuals. Such arrangements, he argues, are the only effective ways of breaking down the sex-role stereotypes into which the nuclear family "tends to force us."

Breaking Up Marriages

Homosexuals now openly devalue marriage and family, proper child-rearing, and heterosexuality by insisting that they, too, are entitled to marry, retain custody of their children after divorce, and to adopt children. A few clergymen and more than a few judges accord them these rights—the clergy believing in the religious entitlement to marriage, the judges either out of fear or because they do not know of persuasive grounds for denying them child custody.

While most homosexuals apparently have not married, numbers of them have been married as bisexuals and had children. Bell and Weinberg reported that almost 20 percent of the male homosexuals and one third of the female homosexuals in their study had been married, some hoping that marriage would somehow cure them of their vice. Those who yield to it ordinarily divorce their spouses, causing tremendous shock and loss.

Their children, for example, somehow try to adjust to a custodial mother who dates women and may have a live-in lesbian lover. Others must visit a homosexual father who has left them and their mother for another man. All such youngsters are unreasonably expected to understand and approve the meaning and implications of a parent's homosexuality. Yet this surely eludes the grasp of younger children, and is by no means well-understood by adolescents—or necessarily accepted by any of them. Indeed, a parent announcing his homosexuality can weaken or badly confuse children's sense of their own gender identity—'will this happen to me?"

Stranding Single Women

The total population of homosexuals is unknown and can only be estimated. If the most commonly mentioned percentage of male and female homosexuals in the population—2 percent (the figure ranges up to 10 percent)—is used, and if the most frequently cited ratio of homosexuality between the sexes (four males to one female) is also accepted, then there are approximately 748,000 male and female homosexuals in the population of unmarried individuals (37.4 million) from age 18 to 64. Of these, slightly more than 598,000 are males and 149,000 are females. Since the latter cancel out the same number of the former, there are about 449,000 male homosexuals who deplete the ranks of marriageable men. Therefore, there are 449,000 marriageable women who will remain single so long as their and the male homosexual populations remain constant.

Not a Natural Occurrence

There is no sound scientific evidence to support the claim that homosexuality is an innate trait; it is a psycho-sexual dysfunction not linked to any known genetic or biological factor.

Enrique T. Rueda and Michael Schwartz, *Gays, AIDS, and You*, 1987.

If the homosexual population is estimated at 3 percent, its total is slightly over 1.22 million, of which almost 890,000 are male and about 220,000 are female. Canceling out the females with an equal number of males results in the balance of nearly 667,000 male homosexuals—the same number of heterosexual females who will, because of this depletion of the population of marriageable males, remain unmarried. Whichever figure is used, a huge number of women are deprived of the opportunity to lead satisfying lives within marriage and family.

Numbers of homosexuals remain religiously observant, and a few Christian and Jewish religious institutions welcome them either by holding special services or establishing special houses of worship for them, or by accepting them into their congregations. Nevertheless, the homosexuals' drive to win moral legitimacy must attempt to render both arbitrary and unjust the religious values underpinning the worthiness of marriage, family, and child-rearing.

Homosexual writers for some time have been critical of Judaism and Christianity because of what C.A. Tripp termed their "reactionary, anti-sexual" moral values. And Dennis Altman complained that "sex has been firmly linked, and nowhere more firmly than in Christian theology, with the institution of the family and with child-bearing. Sex is thus legitimized for its utilitarian principles, rather than as an end in itself, and marriage becomes a 'sacred partnership' entered into for the begetting of children. Even where sexual pleasure is accepted as a complementary goal, the connection between marriage and sex remains." Outraged by the religious support given to marriage and family at the expense of mere sexuality, homosexual writers argued for recognizing the "bisexual needs of human beings," and they bemoan the fact that Greek paganism, with its more open-minded view of homosexuality, was ever supplanted by Christianity and Judaism.

The kind of polymorphous sexuality to which [they] refer is truly typical only of very young children (who outgrow it). As far as scientific evidence goes, human beings have neither polymorphous nor bisexual *needs*. Yet, nothing seems to deter homosexuals from arguing as they wish to convince society that their goal of attaining moral approbation for perversion is a just one. This has been made all the easier for them with the waning influence of religion in an age when unbridled relativism and a narcissistic individualism have become the reigning standards.

"AIDS is God's punishment for homosexual behavior. We may cringe at this notion, but we cannot dispute it."

Homosexuality Is To Blame for AIDS

Billy James Hargis

Billy James Hargis publishes *Christian Crusade*, a newsletter that works to "preserve the faith and save America." In the following viewpoint, excerpted from this newsletter, Hargis contends that God created AIDS to punish homosexuals for their immoral behavior. Innocent people are also dying of AIDS because of homosexuals' sins, he argues.

As you read, consider the following questions:

1. How does Hargis explain the AIDS epidemic in relation to the prophecies of the Bible?
2. Why does Hargis object to "doing your own thing"?
3. According to the author, how can Christians help those afflicted with AIDS?

Billy James Hargis, "AIDS: Sign of the Times!" *Christian Crusade*, Vol. 34, No. 5, 1987. Reprinted with permission.

There are many, including this writer, who believe that AIDS, as well as herpes, is a result of the judgment of God on a nation which has despised His stern commandments regarding sex. As a firm believer in the teachings of the apostle Paul in Ephesians 2:8-9: "For by grace are ye saved through faith; and that not of yourself: it is the gift of God: not of works, lest any man should boast," I therefore believe that sinners can be forgiven of any sin—adultery, homosexuality, divorce, murder, sex, gossip, theft, lying, etc.—and still go to heaven because Jesus once and for all stood in judgment on our behalf in order that we will never have to stand in judgment for our sins. However, I believe that it is scriptural to say that we will pay in this life for the "deeds done in our body." Let me repeat that I believe that each of us can be forgiven of any sin that we commit in this life by believing in the death, burial and resurrection of Christ and keeping His commandments, but I also believe that we will still suffer the consequences in this life for our sins, disobedience, lawlessness and for all the evil deeds done in our body. It would seem that all of us would rather suffer the consequences of our wrongdoing in this life than to spend eternity in hell.

In recent years, there has been the rise of seemingly incurable venereal diseases among couples involved in promiscuous sex, extramarital relationships, fornication and adultery—in other words, heterosexuals caught up in the sexual revolution. Couples involved in frequent promiscuous sex are likely to contract herpes. There is no known cure for this disease.

The Current Problem

Also, male homosexuals, who have insisted on practicing sexual perversion and deviation, have become in increasing number, victims of AIDS. AIDS is the disease which destroys the immune system of the human body and cannot be treated. Any student of the scriptures must concede that God Almighty put the immune system into our bodies in order to enable us to fight many diseases. That was part of His creation of man.

Dr. Dale Crowley said: "This AIDS plague is a shout from heaven, saying, 'You've gone too far.'" As the Lord speaks in judgment, the guilty must suffer, and many innocent along with the guilty. AIDS is undoubtedly one of the last plagues. The end of our age is near.

"Authorities want $2 billion a year to fight AIDS. What is needed, beyond everything else, is to repent and get right with God. For 'God is not willing that any should perish, but that all should come to repentance.'" (II Peter 3:9)

Some disagree with this conclusion that herpes and AIDS is the judgment of God upon unrepentant sinners, by saying that many non-homosexuals have also contracted AIDS although they are not guilty of any wrongdoing. The Lord Jesus Christ told us 2,000 years ago that: "It rains upon the just and the unjust alike." The sins of a few compared to the whole, can cause an epidemic among the masses who become their innocent victims. This is not the fault of God. Instead it is the fault of those who sinned, and who inflicted their fellow human beings with this dreadful plague.

Doing Their Own Thing

Today, every effort is being made to hold those involved in the sexual revolution, either in the practice of promiscuous sex or sexual deviation, as innocent. "They were merely doing their own thing"—they had no intention of involving others. Adolf Hitler was an individual who was doing his own thing, too, but in so doing many millions of innocent people died. There is no way to separate the results of sin from a sinful few and the other fellow human beings who live on this mother earth. Don't blame God because a little child somewhere is dying of AIDS that he got from a needle during treatment or surgery in a hospital. If anyone is to blame, it is the person who spread the disease or the hospital staff member who was responsible for giving the child an injection of medication or a transfusion with a diseased needle.

Bob Dix. Reprinted with permission.

Only those who are involved in the actual sin or crime are guilty. These innocent children are not guilty. Then someone says, "What about the woman whose husband has infected her with AIDS?"

The sin is of the man who infected her. The sin is not hers. But, it rains on the just and the unjust. All of this debate about an unmerciful God, is not going to change that. We are agents of free choice. We can choose to do right, or we can choose to do wrong. Our actions affect others . . . on and on and on. These growing epidemics called AIDS and HERPES, are proof positive that you cannot do your own thing. In wrongdoing, we affect the lives of others. There is no way to avoid this. We can affect others with good and we can affect others with bad. If we cannot check our ungodly sexual lusts, then not only should we expect the consequences, but others will also suffer, and perhaps die, because of our sin.

The Judgment Issue

However, having said this, and before having established the Bible's teaching concerning sin in today's unredeemed world, I must agree with an editorial in Billy Graham's *Christianity Today* of March 20, 1987, under the title, "The Judgment Mentality," that "it is not our job to make AIDS victims feel worse." Here are some quotes from the article:

> The numbers boggle the mind as much as they terrify it. As of November of 1986, 24,011 cases of AIDS had been reported in this country, claiming 13,372 lives (the remainder are almost certain to meet the same fate). The U.S. Public Health Service believes the number of people with AIDS will increase to 270,000 by 1991. And Surgeon General C. Everett Koop projects the number of people worldwide who will die from AIDS could reach 100 million by the end of the century unless a cure is found.

> But as incomprehensible as these figures are, they also invite speculation, especially among Christians. In fact, the urge to speculate has been almost irresistible. Why? The main way to get AIDS is to commit a certain kind of sin. In the U.S., about 73 percent of the people diagnosed with AIDS are homosexual and bisexual males. Hence, the speculation: Is the deadly disease God's judgment on homosexuals?

> Already, a number of articles have appeared in conservative Christian publications suggesting AIDS is God's punishment for homosexual behavior. We may cringe at this notion, but we cannot dispute it. The Bible condemns homosexual acts as sin, and the wages of sin is always death. God's holy anger is set against all sin. He will not be trifled with and he will not be mocked. What we sow we will reap—if not now, certainly in eternity.

> God may indeed be using AIDS to confront homosexuals with their sin. And since the disease is spreading to the heterosexual population, God may also be confronting all forms of promiscuity. There is literally no such thing anymore as "safe sex" outside the boundaries of marriage as God intended it. AIDS could be one dramatic method God is using to wake up a sinful society to the realities of sin and judgment.

I agree with William Cowper: "God moves in mysterious ways, his wonders to perform." Despite the problems I have with the idea, God might be judging sexual sins with AIDS.

It is not our job as Christians to make dying people feel worse. It is our job to give them hope and healing in the name of Christ. We have a wonderful opportunity to give the victims of AIDS simple human compassion and much, much more. We can give them not just a feeling of heaven, but heaven itself. We can give them hope in the mercy and forgiveness of God.

"Homosexuality, promiscuity and drug abuse cannot cause AIDS."

Homosexuality Is Not To Blame for AIDS

Charley Shively

The weekly newspaper *Gay Community News* has served the homosexual population of Boston since the early 1970s, and has run many stories on AIDS since the onset of the epidemic. In the following viewpoint, *Gay Community News* writer Charley Shively argues that homosexuals are being accused unjustly of causing AIDS. Shively contends that America is so busy blaming the victims of AIDS that it is not doing enough to ensure that affordable treatment is available for all who need it.

As you read, consider the following questions:

1. According to the author, how do the attacks on homosexuals function as a smoke screen?
2. Why does Shively believe heterosexuals blame the victims of AIDS?
3. Why would it be unwise for homosexuals to appeal to heterosexuals for sympathy, according to the author?

Charley Shively, "AIDS and Genes: AIDS as Psychological Warfare," *Gay Community News*, October 11-17, 1987. Reprinted with permission.

AIDS is a disease. The psychological warfare of politician, priest and doctor would interpret it as a punishment for homosexuality. Michael Bronski early exposed the redundancy in the term "gay disease"; "gay" and "disease" have long been synonymous. For some heterosexuals, our death is our cure. For some homosexuals, the cure is abstinence. Recently one gay man said AIDS has made us "better." AIDS has not made anyone "better"—unless you believe the only good homosexual is a dead one.

The media (even gay or liberal outlets) exclude any explanation of AIDS that does not scapegoat gay people and drug-users. All the lessons have been lost about the way moralism has prevented control of syphilis and gonorrhea. Few have heeded the message of the 1985 editorial in the *Journal of the Royal Society of Medicine*: "homosexuality, promiscuity and drug abuse cannot cause AIDS. . . ." If promiscuity is not responsible, then we would have to speculate on the origin of the disease. Such speculation has been discouraged if not prohibited.

The CDC [Centers for Disease Control] reported in June of 1981 that five young men had died in Los Angeles of pneumocystis carinii, a form of pneumonia common in very elderly people. The CDC speculated that the fact that "these patients were all homosexuals suggests an association between some aspect of a homosexual lifestyle or disease acquired through sexual contact and pneumocystis pneumonia in this population." While the original label of "gay related immune deficiency" (GRID) didn't last, gay men have become the drunk drivers of this disease. Others, like hemophiliacs, are innocent victims.

A Smoke Screen

Attacking gay men for their promiscuity diverts attention from the question of who controls the chemicals and the genetics. Capital is clearly the correct answer. The great hospitals and research institutions are financed entirely by industry and the government. The interlock between drug companies, hospitals, military research facilities and universities is very tight. Universities have had qualms about the business-research link, but they have resolved the question largely in favor of business. Thus MIT [Massachusetts Institute of Technology] has a semi-autonomous Whitehead Institute. "Super Stocks for Tomorrow: Biotechnology: The Promise and the Perils," an article for entrepreneurs, reports "about 300 U.S. companies are in the biotechnology business today, including the 60 or so whose shares are publicly traded. In addition, nearly every major pharmaceutical house and a number of oil, glass, chemical, computer and other producers are involved in some kind of biotech research or commercial venture." (*Changing Times*, June 1987)

Dr. Robert Gallo's patent on the human immunodeficiency virus will bring in millions of dollars. While he claims the money will go to research, that research will be under his control and directed toward profits. Ronald Reagan himself personally negotiated a settlement with the prime minister of France concerning the proprietary rights to the HIV patent. And the administration has been pushing mandatory testing; with each test profits pour in.

Praying for a Cure

I must address the position that AIDS is a visitation of God's chastisement, though I have little patience with such a homophobic prejudice. Suffice it to say that I pray regularly for a cure to AIDS. I cannot believe that the answer to my prayer will thwart the will of God.

Richard T. Hawkins, *The Witness*, March 1988.

The prerequisite for any treatment of AIDS must be that it will be profitable. Biogenetic products such as Interleuken II is an example; this blood product inspires the investors. *Changing Times* is bullish: "In the U.S. alone, IL-2 sales are projected at $200 million a year by 1990." Since AIDS is a national emergency, drugs that might be useful should be provided at cost. Drug companies, however, routinely engage in price gouging. The price of AZT, one possibly useful drug, has been increased many times since it was tentatively approved for people with AIDS (PWAs). And AL721 (egg lecithin) initially discouraged drug companies because it was so inexpensive. Some companies are putting out the product without testing for potential bacterial, fungal or other contaminants. And most are charging many, many times the cost of production.

Blaming the Victim

Uncritical of those who have profited from AIDS, the government along with the clinics/hospitals/public health groups and religious leaders—from the Pope to Jerry Falwell—have blamed homosexual promiscuity for the disease. They have more or less echoed President Reagan's speech writer: "Call it nature's retribution, God's will, the wages of sin, paying the piper, ecological kickback, whatever phraseology you prefer. The facts demonstrate that promiscuous homosexual conduct is utterly destructive of human health." Calling AIDS a "natural sanction," the Vatican Office of Social Communication said, "Some diseases or physical conditions are the direct result of personal actions, like a hangover or venereal disease." Like Daniel Defoe in *A Journal of the Plague Year* (1721) they have blamed the victims: "There was a seeming propensity or a wicked inclination in those that were infected to infect others."

Displacement of responsibility for illness and mortality is quite common. Thus it is argued that failure to seek medical care explains the high infant and mother mortality rates among the poor, when the real problems are malnutrition, poor housing, and inadequate living standards. During the Bubonic Plague, Jews, because they kept cats, were accused of bewitching Christians, who then killed both the cats and the Jews in order to counter the disease. During the auto heyday of the '50s, automobile deaths were defined as "accidents" and blamed on those killed. Consumer activists have only partially corrected this "accident" construct. Highway deaths are seldom blamed on faulty automobiles, lousy engineering, poor roadways or inadequate public transportation. If not completely "accidental," then casualties are blamed on the driver—particularly the drunk or drugged driver. Mothers Against Drunk Drivers (MADD) don't call for free public transportation; instead they blame drunk drivers, who bring sorrow to mothers, children and other innocent victims.

Exaggerating the Epidemic

John Mitzel (author of *Boston Sex Scandal*) early identified AIDS as the "disease straight people like to talk about." Every effort has been made to exaggerate the extent of the disease. Statistics are reported not on the number of deaths or newly-diagnosed PWAs per year (or per 100,000 people), but instead on the total numbers who have been diagnosed since 1979. Several thousand U.S. deaths per year in a population of over two hundred million cannot be compared with the plague, smallpox, cholera, yellow fever, tuberculosis or even the 1918 Spanish flu. Nonetheless, AIDS is continually compared to such epidemics. Nor can the AIDS death rate be compared to that from cancer, heart disease or automobile accidents.

Since the numbers for AIDS are relatively small, alarmists resort to projections. After I protested in 1982 that the numbers do not justify calling AIDS an "epidemic," one gay leader claimed that epidemics are classified according to rate of increase. No PWAs in 1978; a few in 1979; 261 in 1980; nearly 1,000 in 1982. At that rate of increase everyone would soon be dead, but the rate of increase soon leveled off. Little publicity has been given to the plateau; in 1985, 9,484 new PWAs were counted; in 1986, 10,021. If the disease is leveling off, projections are not. "Federal scientists project that by the end of 1991, total cases will reach 270,000 with 179,000 deaths (NY *Times*, March 16, 1987)."

Homosexuals may be one of the only groups in history to embrace a disease and call it their own. Haitians, when they were listed as a "high risk" group, protested and were able to have themselves excluded from the statistics. Africans have almost universally disclaimed the disease. Only a tiny minority of homosexuals have tried to escape the disease label and pin the guilt on intravenous drug users. (The CDC, in cataloguing people with AIDS, asks first if the person is a homosexual, second about IV drug use, then about hemophilia. Thus a Haitian, hemophiliac, IV drug-using homosexual would only be listed as a homosexual in the statistics.)

Free from Blame

People now suffering from AIDS were, for the most part, infected before much was known about the disease. The epidemic was un-preventable. Care for people who suffer directly or indirectly from AIDS needs to be completely free of blaming the victim. How can people be blamed for behavior they couldn't have known was risking infection?

Gail Hovey, *Christianity and Crisis*, February 15, 1988.

AIDS has become the gay stigmata: by suffering we prove we are worthwhile people. (By enjoying our sexuality, we demonstrate our evil.) The straight world may not be willing to accept us as happy and gay in our sexuality, but trying to overcome that homophobia by appealing for their sympathy is a great betrayal of ourselves. Ann Douglas in her study of women and Protestant ministers in the nineteenth century lays out some of the traps in the appeal for sympathy strategy:

> To stress their ill health was a way for both [women and ministers] to dramatize their anxiety that their culture found them useless and wished them no good; it supplied them, moreover, with a means of getting attention, of obtaining psychological and emotional power even while apparently acknowledging the biological correlatives of their social and political unimportance. *The Feminization of American Culture* (1977).

Unfortunately, some gay people have seen this loathsome disease as a means of redemption, a method of reconciliation with doctors, ministers and politicians. Those who think we will be hated less if we are disabled, have sadly misjudged the compassion of our enemies. The sentimentalist might embrace (while cruising) women, children and ministers, but they fear touching sodomites in any form—able or disabled.

"Far from being sick, gays often function better than nongays."

Homosexuals Contribute to Society

Mark Freedman

Mark Freedman is a founder of the Association of Gay Psychologists and a former staff psychologist at the Northeast Community Mental Health Center in San Francisco. He has published several books on psychological topics including *Personal Definition and Psychological Function.* In the following viewpoint, he discusses some of the research that has been done with gay people showing them to be as mentally healthy as the general population.

As you read, consider the following questions:

1. What evidence does Freedman offer to show that gays often function better than nongays?
2. What does he mean by the term "centering"?
3. In what ways does he believe that "deviation from stereotyped sex roles is a very good thing"?

Ten years ago the word "homosexual" conjured up images of sad, neurotic deviants. But the open spirit of the last decade has improved our knowledge, and a clear picture of homosexuals today would show a great many men and women who live by their own values and whose emotional expressions aren't limited by traditional sex roles. Far from being sick, gays often function *better* than nongays. . . .

Traditionally, psychiatrists have based their view of homosexuality either on armchair speculation or on the analysis of homosexuals who enter therapy—a highly unrepresentative sample. It wasn't until 1957, in fact, that psychologist Evelyn Hooker of UCLA published the first really sound research on the personal adjustment of gay men. Hooker compared homosexuals and heterosexuals who were *not* in therapy after dividing them up into pairs of comparable age, intelligence and schooling and then giving them a battery of personality tests. Experienced clinical psychologists then rated each person's test results without knowing the man's sexual orientation.

Homosexual Disease?

It turned out that the judges couldn't separate homosexuals from heterosexuals any better than if they had simply flipped a coin. The ratings of the homosexuals weren't significantly different from those of the heterosexuals, and about two thirds of both groups seemed to have normal personalities.

Hooker drew several tentative conclusions from her study. First, the clinical entity of "disease" called homosexuality does not exist. The forms of homosexual experience are as varied as the forms of heterosexual experience. Second, homosexuality may well be a deviation that is within the normal range of human behavior. And third, particular forms of sexual desires and expression may play a less important role in personality structure than many psychiatrists assume. Subsequent studies confirm Hooker's finding.

Unfortunately, most of these experiments used male subjects, so I decided in 1967 to do my doctoral research on female homosexuals. My results show that by several different measures of personality, lesbians are no more neurotic or disturbed than heterosexual women.

But there was something else in the test results, something provocative on the face of it: in certain ways, the lesbians actually functioned better than the controls. . . .

Many gay people have responded to social pressures against homosexuality by "centering," by discovering and living according to their own values. An intense quest for identity, purpose and meaning often begins quite early, certainly by the time young homosexuals begin to appreciate the tremendous social pressures against them.

My research on lesbians found them scoring higher than a control group on autonomy, spontaneity, orientation toward the present (as opposed to being obsessed with the past or anticipating the future), and sensitivity to one's own needs and feelings. . . .

I've met a good number of gay people, men and women, who have centered. They don't reject all social conventions and mores, but rather choose among them and develop new patterns of behavior to substitute for whatever they reject. . . .

Feelings of separateness have led some gay people to oppose the values and institutions of the dominant society. The point to recognize here isn't merely the *fact* of alienation but the consciousness of it, a consciousness that can lead naturally to creative responses. The same process occurs among the members of other minority groups that must endure discrimination. Among homosexuals, I believe, creative opposition has produced not only new social concepts but an increased sensitivity to the value of the individual person in our society.

Sex Roles

Besides centering, there are two other ways in which some gays function better than nongays: sex roles may be more egalitarian and sexuality more expressive. . . . Conventional views of sex roles are too narrow to be healthy. In some cases, deviation from stereotyped sex roles is a very good thing. Research and my own experience have convinced me that many gays show a wider range of emotional expression because they are not confined by the standard roles. Lesbians, for instance, may show "masculine"attributes such as assertiveness and aggression. My research also indicates that lesbians *accept* their natural aggressive feelings better than their heterosexual counterparts, and tend to seek the kinds of satisfaction from their work that men do. As for gay men, they're more able to express "feminine" emo-

Mike Peters, *Dayton Daily News.* Reprinted with permission.

tions such as tenderness and even frank weakness than most non-gay men. . . .

The shared wisdom of the gay world is that two men or two women living together as mates quickly see the limitations of stereotyped sex roles. Breadwinner/homemaker and dominant/submissive dichotomies just aren't as important to gays as they are to most people. Obviously, there are a great many exceptions to this tendency, but the point I am trying to make is that homosexuality *in some cases* leads to better-than-average functioning and to a fuller realization of certain fundamental values. . . .

Society's picture of the homosexual often includes an image of furtiveness, of tortured secrecy. There is obvious truth to this stereotype. After all, homosexuals have commonly been rejected by their families, fired from their jobs, dishonorably discharged from military service and even beaten when their sexual orientation came to light. As a consequence, most gays have been forced to hide behind a mask of heterosexuality in order to survive. This situation can make a person acutely unhappy. But it can also lead to certain responses that are not only healthy but sometimes unusually satisfying.

For one thing, gay people in hiding may become quite sophisticated about the masks people wear—about the relationship, that is, between identity and role. This is a useful sensitivity.

Coming Out

There are also advantages in "coming out," in announcing one's homosexuality. Openness about being gay is a process of self-disclosure that a person can control; and many gays have a fairly complex understanding of self-disclosure, both in themselves and others. Moreover, they are often more candid and open than nongays. My own research, which used the Eysenck Personality Inventory among other tests, showed that the lesbian group told fewer lies than the heterosexual controls. They were more candid and less defensive. William Horstman in 1972 reached the same conclusion about men when he matched the MMPI scores of 50 homosexual and 50 heterosexual men. The homosexuals scored lower in lies.

The healthy attributes I've mentioned—centering, transcendence of sex roles, freer sexuality and candor—are probably the result of personality development as well as social pressure. I am not saying that millions of gay people in this country always function better than heterosexuals. The true picture is more complicated than that. . . .

Gay people are different from other people and it would be silly to deny it. Exactly how all the differences develop is not yet clear; complex patterns of social learning probably account for most of them. What I have tried to show here, though, is that these differences reveal some extremely positive aspects of homosexuality. Gay people constitute a large and varied group, and they are capable of proving new kinds of personal fulfillment and social vitality.

"Psychiatrists have ceased calling homosexuality a sickness, or a lack, but one is not sure that they— or others—have ceased thinking that way about it (or that they should.)"

Homosexuals Harm Society

Michael Novak

Michael Novak, a prolific conservative writer, theologian and philosopher, is the author of several books including *Belief and Unbelief, The Rise of the Unmeltable Ethnics* and *The Joy of Sports*. His many articles have appeared in such publications as *Christianity and Crisis* and *National Review*. Novak has taught at the State University of New York and has been the Associate Director for Humanities of the Rockefeller Foundation. In the following viewpoint, he explains why he believes that homosexuality is abnormal and a detriment to society.

As you read, consider the following questions:

1. According to Novak, what is "the male principle"?
2. What aspects of society undermine the male principle, in the author's opinion?
3. Why does Novak believe homosexuality detracts from society?

Michael Novak, "Men Without Women," *The American Spectator*, October 1978. Copyright 1978 *The American Spectator*.

In past ages, homosexuality was sometimes construed as a danger to the human race because it meant a) a decline in population, or b) a decline in those masculine qualities essential for survival. What happened in the socialization of the young male was perceived to be of greater significance, and of greater risk, to the race than what happened to the female. Unless I am mistaken, even today society is in a more troubled state about male homosexuality than about female homosexuality. Lesbianism may suggest infantile pleasure and regression, but it does not threaten the public, at least not to the same extent that male homosexuality does. . . .

Decline of Male Principle

Female homosexuality seems somehow more natural, perhaps harmless. Male homosexuality seems to represent a breakdown of an important form of socialization.

The point may need elaboration. Recent publicity about women has served to shield us from an event of far greater significance: the decline of value, status, and the need of "masculine" qualities. In modern corporate life, "mother bureaucracy" swallows the strong ego. Rewards do not come from taking risks, being aggressive, speaking out. In the rationalized, smooth world of government and corporate life, "going along to get along" wins more certain rewards.

The rules of corporate bureaucracy may be more decisive in altering sex roles than the pill. These rules weaken masculine qualities. . . .

The modern era suffocates the male principle. (I say "male" rather than "masculine" to emphasize the high animal spirits involved, the instinctual base on which culture works.) The deep and wide-ranging changes in our experience of maleness have been too little explored. They have certainly induced vast sexual confusion. . . .

Is it true that the number of homosexuals is multiplying in our day? Who could marvel if it were? Men find it perplexing to be male. . . .

It is not just that "sex-role stereotypes" are breaking down. Rather, basic systems of identity have been profoundly altered by the technology and organization of modern life. Personal confusion abounds. The problem is deeper than that of homosexuality alone.

Society has a special stake in the development of married family life. Without strong, enlightened, spiritually nourishing families, the future of society looks bleak indeed. The family is the original, and still the most effective, department of health, education, and welfare. If it fails to teach honesty, courage, a desire for excellence, and a whole host of basic skills, it is exceedingly difficult for any other agency to make up for its failure. . . .

In addition, the raising of children is morally demanding in a special way. Most of what one learns is failure. A raw realism develops. The brute demands of running a house, of keeping order, of teaching all that one must teach, and of encountering the daily struggles of self-will and self-assertion on the part of each parent and each child are of great moral significance. . . .

From my point of view, homosexuals absent themselves from the most central struggles of the individual, the struggle to enter into communion with a person of the opposite sex. That is the battle most at the heart of life. Excluded from this struggle, whether by choice or by psychic endowment, the homosexual is deprived of its fruits. Those fruits are a distinctive honesty, realism and wisdom taught by each sex to the other: that complementarity in which your humanity is rejoined and fulfilled. Apart from this civilizing struggle there is a lack, an emptiness, a loss of realism. . . .

Unnatural Homosexuality

Homosexuality is, in a certain sense, unnatural. . . . I use the term "natural" here to mean "appropriate to the nature of man," for I am at a loss to know what other term to use in dealing with the obvious fact that human bodies seem more obviously designed for heterosexual intercourse than for homosexual, both as to technique and to purpose. . . .

And it seems to me that one cannot honestly ignore the relation of sex to reproduction. . . . The fact is that homosexuality generally entails a renunciation of responsibility for the continuance of the human race and of a voice in the dialogue of the generations. . . . It is harder to live a complete life than a partial one, and easier to life in fantasy than in reality.

Samuel McCracken, *Commentary*, January 1979.

Psychiatrists have ceased calling homosexuality a sickness, or a lack, but one is not sure that they—or others—have ceased thinking that way about it (or that they should). There are three features in the very structure of homosexual life that tell against it. The first is a preoccupation with one's own sex. Half the human mystery is evaded. The second is the instability of homosexual relationships, an instability that arises from the lack of the full dimension of raising a family. Apart from having and raising children, a couple can hardly help a degree of self-preoccupation. The structure of family life—the same onerous structure that feels like a "trap"—places the married couple in a context larger than themselves, shields them from one another, so to speak, and opens up new avenues of realism and honesty. It is an especially important experience to exercise the authority of a parent, having rebelled against mother, or father, or both, for so many years. Only thus does one see things from the other side.

Thirdly, the homosexual faces a particular sort of solipsism, which is difficult to escape simply through companionship. Homesexual love is somehow apart from the fundamental mystery of bringing life into the world, and sharing in the birth and death of the generations. It is self-centered in a way that is structural, independent of the goodwill of the individual. Marital love has a structural role in continuing the human race that is independent of the failures of the individuals who share it.

There are also particular dangers in homosexuality. If it is true that the homosexual is lacking something that nature usually intends, then that lack is bound to be felt, at least unconsciously. A certain rage against nature is likely to be felt, and perhaps internalized and directed at the self. Of course, it is often argued that nature has made no mistake, that the homosexual is fully endowed, and that it is *society* that is the cheat. The rage will then be directed against society. . . .

Society's Interests

Society has a strong interest, in private and in public, in encouraging heterosexuality and in discouraging homosexuality. . . .

I am in favor of a tolerant and open system. I am not in favor of one that treats heterosexuality and homosexuality as equals, or as matters of indifference. Individuals (and societies) can make their own moral vision clear without undue coercion upon those who do not, or who cannot, share it. For the good of all of us, homosexuals included, it is well that society should prefer heterosexuality and specially nourish it. The future depends on it.

a critical thinking activity

Recognizing Stereotypes

A stereotype is an oversimplified or exaggerated description of people or things. Stereotyping can be favorable. However, most stereotyping tends to be highly uncomplimentary and, at times, degrading.

Stereotyping grows out of our prejudices. When we stereotype someone, we are prejudging him or her. Consider the following example: Mr. Smith believes that all homosexuals are promiscuous and incapable of committed love. The possibility that some homosexuals have long-term or life-long monogamous relationships does not occur to him. He has prejudged all homosexuals and will not recognize any possibility which is not consistent with his belief.

The following statements relate to the subject matter in this chapter. Consider each statement carefully. *Mark S for any statement that is an example of stereotyping. Mark N for any statement that is not an example of stereotyping. Mark U if you are undecided about any statement.*

If you are doing this activity as a member of a class or group, compare your answers with those of other class or group members. Be able to defend your answers. You may discover that others will come to different conclusions than you do. Listening to the reasons others present for their answers may give you valuable insights in recognizing stereotypes.

S = *stereotype*
N = *not a stereotype*
U = *undecided*

83

1. All homosexual men are obsessed with sex.

2. Numbers of homosexuals remain religiously observant.

3. It is well known that homosexual couples are not faithful to each other.

4. AIDS researchers are profit-hungry and greedy.

5. Gay men are naturally artistic.

6. Dörner saw homosexuality as something to be purged from human life by stopping it before it formed.

7. Scientists estimate that between two and ten percent of the population is homosexual.

8. All homosexual men had domineering mothers and weak fathers.

9. Homosexual men wish they were women.

10. Lesbians have masculine personality traits, such as assertiveness and courage.

11. The government, religious leaders, and public health officials are all looking for a scapegoat on which to blame the AIDS epidemic. Homosexuals have become that scapegoat.

12. Homosexuality was once thought to be a sign of mental illness.

13. Psychiatrists are biased against homosexuals.

14. The number of homosexuals in America may be multiplying.

15. Homosexuals hate the traditional family because they are completely locked out of it.

16. The straight world needs to accept that homosexuals can be happy with their orientation.

17. Homosexual practices can spread AIDS.

18. The Bible condemns homosexuality as a sin. It also says that those who sin will die.

19. Those who oppose homosexuality are religious bigots.

20. Lesbians are more comfortable with their own sexuality than heterosexual women are.

Periodical Bibliography

The following articles have been selected to supplement the diverse views presented in this chapter.

Gary Atkins   "Forced March in the Military," *The Nation*, January 2, 1989.

C. Donald Cole   "The Church and Homosexuals," *Moody Monthly*, November 1988.

Michael H. Hodges   "No Gays, Please, We're British," *The Nation*, February 6, 1989.

Jonathan Ned Katz   "Gay Couples Deserve the Rights and Benefits of Partnership," *Civil Liberties*, Winter 1988. Available from the American Civil Liberties Union, 132 W. 43rd St., New York, NY 10036.

James J. Kilpatrick   "Homosexual Soldiers: What Are Their Rights?" *Conservative Chronicle*, March 2, 1988. Available from Hampton Publishing Co., Box 29, Hampton, IA 50441.

Henry Klingeman   "Anonymous Sex," *National Review*, June 19, 1987.

Melvin Konner   "Homosexuality: Who and Why?" *The New York Times Magazine*, April 2, 1989.

Jim Lynch   "Witch Hunt at Parris Island," *The Progressive*, March 1989.

D. Keith Mano   "Arresting Gays," *National Review*, October 28, 1988.

James Merrett   "Keep Momma from the Truth," *The Advocate*, August 30, 1988. Available from Liberation Publications, Inc., 6922 Hollywood Blvd., Tenth Floor, Los Angeles, CA 90022.

National Review   "Tragic Confusion," March 13, 1987.

Charles E. Rice   "Uncle Sam Doesn't Want Them," *The New American*, March 28, 1988.

Scott Schrader   "Get Thee Behind Me, Homosexuality," *The Advocate*, January 17, 1989. Available from Liberation Publications, Inc., 6922 Hollywood Blvd., Tenth Floor, Los Angeles, CA 90022.

Is Sex Education
Beneficial?

SEXUAL
VALUES

Chapter Preface

Although sex education is taught in many of America's schools, controversy about it continues to rage. Opinions on sex education range from the belief that America should have more of it to the belief that it should be abolished.

Those who believe teenagers need more sex education argue that teens should be advised to refrain from sex, but that it is unrealistic to believe that even the majority will do so. Thus it is essential that they be given instruction on contraceptive use in order to reduce the number of unwanted teen pregnancies that occur each year. They contend that sex education is particularly urgent in the age of AIDS, when ignorance of the means of preventing transmission of the disease, combined with sexual experimentation, could be fatal.

Opponents of sex education believe it harms teenagers. Teens, they say, should be told unequivocally to refrain from sex before marriage. By teaching contraception, schools are tacitly condoning premarital sex. These opponents also believe that sex education actually increases teen pregnancy because it encourages teens to experiment with sex.

The fact that both sides wish to do what is best for teenagers makes this emotional argument all the more heated. In the following chapter, sex education is examined closely.

"Sexuality education can help enhance physical and mental health and promote greater communication and caring within our society."

Sex Education Is Beneficial

Diane deMauro and Debra Haffner

Diane deMauro and Debra Haffner write for SIECUS, the Sex Information and Education Council of the United States. SIECUS was founded in 1964 and is one of the nation's largest clearinghouses for information on sexuality. In the following viewpoint, deMauro and Haffner answer common questions about sex education. They argue that sex education is beneficial because it increases the use of contraceptives and decreases unwanted pregnancies among teenagers.

As you read, consider the following questions:

1. According to the authors, why do most parents welcome sex education in the schools?
2. Does sex education work, according to deMauro and Haffner?
3. What topics do deMauro and Haffner believe most parents want sex education classes to teach?

Excerpts from "Sexuality Education and the Schools: Issues and Answers" by Diane de Mauro and Debra Haffner, published in 1988 by SIECUS. Copyright © Sex Information and Education Council of the U.S., Inc., New York, NY.

What is sexuality education?

Sexuality education is a lifelong process of acquiring information and forming attitudes, beliefs, and values about identity, relationships, and intimacy.

Sexuality education is more than teaching young people about anatomy and the physiology of reproduction. It includes an understanding of sexuality in its broadest context—sexual development, reproductive health, interpersonal relationships, affection and intimacy, body image, and sex and gender roles.

Who teaches sexuality education?

Parents are the primary sexuality educators of their children. Infants and toddlers receive this education when parents talk to them, dress them, show affection, play with them, and teach them the names of the parts of their bodies. As children grow, they continue to receive messages about appropriate behaviors and values as they develop relationships within their family and the social environment. Children learn about sexuality through their observations and relationships with parents, friends, teachers, and neighbors; television, music, books, advertisements, and toys teach them about sexual issues.

It is important, however, that the process of sexual learning within the family be supplemented by planned learning opportunities in churches and synagogues, community and youth agencies, and schools.

Learning About Sex

What about school-based sexuality education?

School-based sexuality education programs conducted by specially trained educators can add an important dimension to children's ongoing sexual learning. These programs should be developmentally appropriate and include such issues as self-esteem, family relationships, parenting, friendships, values, communication techniques, dating, and decision-making skills. Programs must be carefully planned by each community in order to respect the diversity of values and beliefs present in a classroom.

Unfortunately, only 10% of school-age youth participate in a comprehensive program lasting at least 40 hours. Although studies indicate that between 60-75% of students receive some type of sexuality education by the time they graduate from high school, fewer than one sixth of schools offer separate sexuality education courses. Even fewer schools offer programs at the elementary level.

How do most people learn about sex?

Recent polls indicate that most young people look to their parents as their most important source of information about sexuality. Friends are the second most important source, school courses rank third and television is fourth. Over two thirds of young people have talked to their parents about sexuality. Among the adults polled, a much smaller number learned about sex from their own parents (21% from their mother; 5% from the father), yet two thirds of these adults indicate that they have talked with their own children about sexual issues. In numerous studies, most parents report that they are uncomfortable discussing such explicit sexual issues as intercourse, masturbation, homosexuality, and orgasm with their children, and welcome assistance from more formal programs.

Bill Sanders, *Milwaukee Journal.* Reprinted with permission.

Why teach sexuality education in schools?

The goals of sexuality education are to promote sexual health and sexuality as a natural part of life. Sexuality education can increase communication skills, enhance self-esteem, facilitate constructive peer exchange and promote positive social, health and developmental outcomes. It can help people to accept themselves and others and to learn to be caring, responsible individuals. Sexuality education can help young people make responsible personal decisions.

Does school-based sexuality education work?

The effectiveness of sexuality education can be me[...] increases in knowledge, attitudinal changes and self-r[...] behavioral changes. School-based programs increase knowle[...] about sexual issues, help teens clarify their values, improve communication with parents and friends, and when combined with a clinic program, facilitate contraceptive use.

Research indicates that young people who have had sex education are no more likely to have sexual intercourse than those who have never taken a course. Among those teenagers who are having sexual intercourse, students who have taken sexuality education classes are significantly more likely to use contraception. Only half of these young women and a third of the men have taken a sexuality education course before they have first coitus.

Innovative programs that combine sexuality education with clinic services and community support may help reduce teenage pregnancy rates. In Baltimore, a school-based education and clinic program led to increases in knowledge about contraception and sexual issues, an increased use of contraception by both males and females, delay in first intercourse, and increased use of family planning clinics. A community based education program with a strong school sex education component in South Carolina reduced the community's teen pregnancy rates. A model program in New York that couples sexuality education with health services, self-esteem enhancement, a sports program, tutoring, and job training, decreased pregnancy rates and increased employment and college enrollment.

From another perspective, the impact of sexuality education may not be quantifiable. Programs can assist children to be more responsible, knowledgeable and confident. Comprehensive sexuality education can help enhance physical and mental health and promote greater communication and caring within our society; it can help the individual understand the consequences of one's actions, make appropriate decisions and develop nonexploitative sexual choices.

The Majority Opinion

Who supports sexuality education?

The vast majority of Americans support sexuality education. A 1985 Harris poll found that 84 percent of adults support sex education. A 1986 *Time* magazine survey found that 95% favor providing facts about AIDS and 89% favor giving information about birth control to individuals over 12. Almost 90% of adults want their children to learn about AIDS, STDs [sexually transmitted diseases], and birth control. Between 70% and 80% of parents want premarital sex, sexual intercourse, abortion and homosexuality discussed in the classroom.

Many youth and community groups as well as professional organizations have adopted policies supportive of sexuality education. . . .

What about government?

There is no national law or policy on sexuality education. At the present time, 13 states plus the District of Columbia, have mandates for sexuality education: Delaware, Georgia, Iowa, Illinois, Kansas, Kentucky, Maryland, Nevada, New Jersey, Rhode Island, South Carolina, Vermont and Virginia. Michigan has proposed a mandate pending final approval. At least 20 other states have guidelines for school health programs including sexuality education as an integral component. However, in many states these mandates preclude the teaching about such subjects as intercourse, abortion, masturbation, and homosexuality. Further, only a few communities have implemented comprehensive school-based education programs at all grade levels that offer young people the opportunity to discuss their feelings, attitudes, and experiences about sexual issues.

Examining Values

America's children and adolescents are not being properly educated about sex. . . . Once sex education encourages young people to examine their values and apply the facts that are being taught, the teenage pregnancy rate and the number of sexually transmitted diseases should decrease.

Cynthia J. Varcoe, *Selected Topics in Human Sexuality*, 1988.

Many states have implemented guidelines or mandates in direct response to the AIDS crisis. According to the National Association of State Boards of Education, at least 24 states and the District of Columbia have mandated AIDS education. The content recommended by these mandates varies dramatically; only a few states have recommended comprehensive programs that provide explicit information about risk reduction.

"Sex education is anathema to normal sexual growth."

Sex Education Is Harmful

Melvin Anchell, interviewed by Paul Fisher

Melvin Anchell is a physician and psychoanalyst who has written on human sexuality, pornography, and sex education. Paul Fisher is the author of *Behind the Lodge Door: Church, State and Freemasonry in America.* The following viewpoint is excerpted from an interview Fisher conducted with Anchell. In it, Anchell contends that sex education is unnecessary, since humans have reproduced for centuries without it. It is also harmful, he argues, because it promotes homosexuality and abortion.

As you read, consider the following questions:

1. What does Anchell believe is the problem with sex education courses?
2. What concepts does Anchell object to in the sex education curriculum?
3. Why does Anchell object to privately-run sex education programs?

Melvin Anchell, interviewed by Paul Fisher, "The Case Against Sex Education," *A.L.L. About Issues,* November/December 1988.

Doctor, my understanding is that most of those in the scientific and medical community favor sex education in the classroom. Why do you oppose such instruction?

I've been asked that question whenever I give a talk. I'm not opposed to anything, but, in explaining my position, I can not give a one sentence answer. Perhaps an analogy will help.

Eliminating sex education from education curricula may be compared to a situation where a physician removes a diseased, abscessed appendix from a child, only to have the parents ask the physician what he will put back into the child's abdomen to replace the diseased appendix.

That's the key, then? Sex education is unnecessary to begin with?

People think that sex education is an integral part of teaching and learning, and that if you remove sex education, you will have created a vacuum in the educational process which must be filled by some other type of sex education course. That idea is completely erroneous.

Sex education is not like reading or writing or other essential skills that have to be taught.

Nature never intended for children to go to school to learn how to mate. And nature never intended that children should be taught from a book how to feel affection.

Unnatural Intrusions

What is the problem with all these courses?

There are two problems with these courses. One, any sex education course must necessarily inject into the sex life of the individual, which is an abnormal thing to do publicly. When you start talking publicly about physical sex you are intruding on the private sex life of individuals, which is against the natural quality of human sexuality.

And what is the second problem you referred to concerning "sex respect" instruction?

Secondly, sex courses can't teach affection.

How did we ever get involved with sex education in this country?

Largely due to the work of Dr. Mary Calderone. For her own reasons, she decided it was necessary to teach young children about sex from kindergarten through high school. By herself, along with some influential followers, she went about this country and in only a few short years established the type of sex education we have today. Her organization was called SIECUS, which means the Sex Information and Education Council of the United States, although it was never a federal government agency, even though the title suggested such was the case.

Once established, she and her colleagues more or less stepped back and passed their sex education ideas to Planned Parenthood and its associated agencies.

What has been her view of the latency period in children?

I began mentioning the latency period occurring in 6 to 12 year olds in 1969. Apparently, I became a thorn in the side of Mary Calderone and SIECUS. After I had done a television show in which I discussed latency at length I noticed about two weeks later that Mary Calderone made a pronunciamento saying that there is no such thing as latency.

Now, latency is an essential psychoanalytical precept. If it were untrue the very keystone from the arch of psychoanalysis would be torn down. Because latency does not augment SIECUS and Planned Parenthood's sex education arguments, they simply declared it doesn't exist.

A NEW 27-MAN COMMITTEE REPORT TO SIR EDWARD BOYLE URGES FULLER SEX INSTRUCTION IN SCHOOLS

BIRDS AND BEES DEPARTMENT

INFORMATION

COMPLAINTS

FRANKLIN

© Franklin/Rothco

Did any of your colleagues in the psychiatric or psychological fraternity support her?

The American Psychiatric Association some years ago claimed that all perversions are normal. That's like putting an atomic bomb in the center of psychoanalytic knowledge and setting it off.

When the American Psychiatric Association announced that all perversions are normal, the Psychoanalytic Association had no way to go up against this very powerful organization. It would be like David going against Goliath.

The Psychoanalytic Society unfortunately assumed the position that it would just sit back and watch the passing parade.

Did the Psychiatric Association statement, which said perversions are normal, give a big boost to people adopting homosexuality and other perverted life styles?

Yes. Doctors, like members of any other organization, essentially are followers. And when prestigious leaders of national medical organizations—people who are presidents, vice presidents, secretaries, and so forth—make major statements, the average physician will follow what the leaders proclaim. . . .

It is obvious that homosexuality has become popular in the wake of the explosive growth of sex education in the classrooms. Is there a cause and effect relationship?

Manuals used in sex education programs sponsored by Planned Parenthod specifically state that homosexuals should be invited into the classrooms. These homosexuals serve as teachers and describe homosexual practices in detail.

What about abortion teachings in sex education classes?

The sex courses provide detailed information on contraception and abortion.

The comments you have made in this interview concerning the harm sex education does to young people represents your professional experience and observations over many years, is that correct?

My experience, yes, as well as observations of other clinicians, reported case histories and some statistical data. Aside from the scientific community, such as medicine and so forth, much can be learned from the written history of people.

🐝 Getting Sex Out of School

It is interesting to note that many religiously-oriented schools, parochial schools, are going along with a lot of unbridled sex education.

In that connection, your idea of control over raw instincts simply is not emphasized enough, even though study after study confirms what you say—it's self-evident.

It's self-evident, therefore it's difficult to explain. Things that are deeply rooted in the mind from the beginning of time should not require lots of explanation.

What can we do about getting sex education out of schools? How do we overcome the power and influence of Planned Parenthood?

Well, we have several weapons. The first of which is *truth.*

The truth of what has been said in my book (*Killers of Children*) should make anyone aware that sex education is anathema to normal sexual growth.

If a person reads that book from the beginning to the end, he or she will need no further explanation. It's all there. Unfortunately, truth is powerful, but fails sometimes to be convincing.

Once people have prejudices, truth and reasoning may not change their biases.

But isn't there a well entrenched prejudice in favor of sex education?

Yes. A rather large number of fathers and mothers have been persuaded by proponents of sex education, that there is a need for sex education. These parents have been persuaded in favor of sex education.

But, as you have noted, won't some people want a sex education program to take the place of Planned Parenthood's offerings?

That's exactly what will happen. While some parents will see that removing Planned Parenthood type sex education from the classroom is a life-sustaining measure, others will continue to feel a need to put some education program into the curriculum to replace it—something they consider more innocuous.

Sex Propaganda

What makes "sex education" a fraud is that its whole thrust is not science but propaganda for new sexual attitudes and lifestyles. It would not take a week, much less a semester, to teach young people the basic biological facts of life. What takes so much time is slowly but steadily undermining the values their parents have taught them and replacing these values with new attitudes that accept adultery, abortion, homosexuality and the rest of the secular religion that calls itself "sex education."

Thomas Sowell, *The Washington Times*, May 17, 1988.

I believe you compare this situation to the efficacy of two poisons.

Exactly. It is true that privately promoted sex programs striving to teach sexual openness along with prudence are preferable to the established SIECUS-Planned Parenthood programs. However, arsenic also is less injurious than cyanide, but neither should be given to students.

Never Necessary

You have noted that since the beginning of time, sex education was never necessary either for microscopic life, like the amoeba, nor for man to reproduce and carry on the species.

Yes. Even the simplest viruses reproduce perfectly without outside help.

Indeed, all creatures in the universe mate and reproduce without ever having to go to school to be taught how.

Let me add: Up until 20 years ago there was no problem with populating the world. There was no problem with people mating. The morality was such that it did not sanction casual affairs, but the ability for people to mate was no less than it is today. As a matter of fact, it was probably greater because there was no sex education interfering with normal sexual growth processes.

Although mating may bring pleasure, the sex act must also have the capability of reproducing if it is to fulfill the needs of the sexual instinct.

Sex Education and Death

It seems that the sex educators' trophy case is filled with abortions, perversions, homosexual activities, venereal disease and suicides. They have nothing to point to with pride.

It hasn't done a thing for enhancing human life. Sex education has such an affinity with death instincts that some schools are beginning to teach students about death. The courses consist of teaching that death, when it comes prematurely, should be accepted with open arms as a great natural gift. As you know, the suicide rate among young people is at an all time high.

You must be a lonely figure taking the positions you do.

That has nothing to do with the truth of what I'm talking about.

Oh, I understand.

And I also understand that you have advocated the revival of a social conscience in our society.

Well, that is really the crux. If a society does not adhere to sexual morality and decency; if it does not agree that sex is an intimate affair; that affection is a vital part of sex—which it is—and if society agrees to accept pornography, live-ins, free love, preteen-teen sex, etc., as a part of its culture then it has reached a serious state of regression.

"It is possible to convince teens to forego early pregnancy and childbearing."

Sex Education Can Reduce Teen Pregnancy

Michael A. Carrera and Patricia Dempsey

Michael A. Carrera is a professor of health sciences at Hunter College in New York City. He is also director of the Teen Primary Pregnancy Prevention Program of The Children's Aid Society, a New York-based agency which offers sex education and other services to improve children's lives. Patricia Dempsey is an assistant professor of social work at Hunter College and program coordinator of the Teen Primary Pregnancy Prevention Program. In the following viewpoint, the authors describe how a comprehensive program that includes sex education, job counseling, health services, and other programs drastically reduces the incidence of teen pregnancy.

As you read, consider the following questions:

1. What do Carrera and Dempsey mean by a holistic approach to preventing teen pregnancy?
2. How does the program mentioned work to prevent teen pregnancy, according to the authors?
3. How successful has this program been, in the authors' opinion?

Reprinted from "Restructuring Public Policy Priorities on Teen Pregnancy" by Michael A. Carrera and Patricia Dempsey, published in 1988 by SIECUS. Copyright © 1988 Sex Information and Education Council of the U.S., Inc., New York, NY.

Each year, more than one million American teenagers become pregnant, the overwhelming majority unintentionally; 44% of these pregnancies result in births. Half of these births are to young women who have dropped out of school and have not yet reached their eighteenth birthdays; 50% are to young women who are not married. Young mothers are at an enormous risk of pregnancy complications and poor birth outcomes, and their infants face greater health and development risks. Teen males, even those who want to be involved, are often forgotten, excused, or written off, and teen marriages, which often compound the problem, are characterized by long-term welfare dependency and family instability. Teenage parents are more likely than those who delay childbearing to experience chronic unemployment, inadequate income, and reduced educational experiences.

Teen pregnancy is a major factor in, and a contributor to, family poverty. One out of every five children are poor; one out of two children is in a female-headed household. The emotional toll on teen parents is staggering, as is society's economic burden in sustaining them. . . .

It is possible to convince teens to forego early pregnancy and childbearing if they have a more hopeful sense of their future. When more hopeful, they, in general, value and have a more positive sense of themselves. They develop appropriate coping skills; become more active and less passive; have more opportunities open up for them; and are more willing to communicate with a concerned adult about their sexuality.

Unfortunately however, many urban teen males and females today do not see any future for themselves: they live in poor communities; they see little employment opportunities; and have little, if any, reason to believe that they will fair as well as, let alone better than, their parents. . . .

One Solution

The Children's Aid Society's Teen Pregnancy Primary Prevention Program has been developed to create a holistic climate in which positive change can occur. To the best of our knowledge, taken altogether, a holistic program such as this—which has been established to serve the west, central, and east Harlem areas of the city of New York—has thus far not been replicated anywhere else in the country.

Our programmatic philosophy is based on the belief that, in order to create a climate where positive change can occur and where direction can be given to young people, it is necessary to influence multiple facets of their lives over a continuous period of time. This holistic type of approach represents a very complex intervention strategy.

Believing that such a comprehensive, quality of life, holistic approach can affect the life options that we seek for young people—even those who live within family systems which have experienced generations of economic deprivation—we have designed our program components to operate concurrently and sometimes simultaneously. These program components center on working with, and affecting, a young person individually, as well as within his or her family and community systems.

The School's Role

Schools certainly can play a role in giving teens the capacity they need to delay pregnancy, through examining and upgrading their teaching of family life and sexuality education, by providing comprehensive school health programs, and by opening their doors to community organizations that want to help teens and their parents get much-needed information, advice, and services.

Children's Defense Fund, *Preventing Adolescent Pregnancy: What Schools Can Do,* September 1986.

The programmatic vision of our Teen Primary Prevention Program is based on several organizing principles. We believe that young people are capable of more than simply avoiding problems and situations which will complicate their lives. We believe that they are capable of "doing good" for themselves, their family, and their community. Our staff's attitudes and behavior sustain this notion and encourage young people to realize their potential for such achievements. This belief affects our entire program.

Preventing Pregnancies

We believe that parents, grandparents, foster parents, and other adults in the community are significant influences on the sexual development of young people. Their roles, therefore should be respected and should be included in holistic, quality-of-life programs—and in meaningful ways.

We believe that people should delay having intercourse, for as long as possible, because intercourse is the kind of special intimacy that best fits a relationship later in life. However, we are mindful that intercourse for some teens is a way of coping with their feelings of poor self-image, fatalism, and unhappiness. Therefore, we are prepared to replace this coping mechanism with options, possibilities, and experiences which are meaningful, which will make sense, and which will also be useful to them at this time in their development.

We are also aware that young people do not always listen to the guidance of adults and may begin to have intercourse—even in their preteen and early teen years. In these situations, our role is to care, to understand, and to try to help them function in a way that will prevent pregnancy. We do not turn our backs or withhold affections as forms of disapproval. Rather, we are present in an ongoing way to provide guidance and on-site contraceptive services, when necessary, so that unintended pregnancy does not occur.

We have discovered, during the first 36 months of our work, that this type of honest and supportive limit-setting approach is appreciated by young people. It helps them to clarify their thoughts and actions much more than the threat-and-fear-arousing communications that have so frequently characterized the way many adults have chosen to relate with young people.

Our pregnancy prevention efforts are addressed equally to both males and females. Our attitude is that males must also be reached, educated, and positively influenced concerning their roles and responsibilities in relationships. To just teach women to say "no" continues a sexist double standard. Teaching young men "not to ask" gives our approach balance and also provides them with an important learning opportunity.

Our Program

The components of our program cover such areas as family life and sex education; physical and mental health services; self-esteem enhancement through the performing arts; lifetime sports; academic assessment and homework-help; job and career awareness; and college admission.

Family Life and Sex Education Program. This is a formal 15-week, two-hours-per-week educational experience for teens and for parents led by the authors who have been certified by the American Association of Sex Educators, Counselors and Therapists. The program centers on an understanding of sexuality from a holistic viewpoint. While there is discussion of sexual anatomy, reproduction, and contraception, more emphasis is placed on exploring such issues as gender roles, family roles, body images, and patterns of affection, love, and intimacy. Roles, responsibilities, and values in relationships are emphasized. Since increasing the sexual literacy of both young people and the adults in their lives is our goal, we have also included readings, films, role-playing, and lectures for both.

Medical and Health Services are provided four hours each week by the center nurse and by adolescent medicine specialists from Montefiore Hospital in the Bronx and Mt. Sinai Hospital in Manhattan. Every teen has a complete annual physical (and every female a yearly GYN examination), preceded by a thorough social and family health inventory. This becomes a valuable part of each teen's health history.

When necessary, physicians provide confidential contraception counseling and prescription. Each youngster—male and female—

who is using a contraceptive has a weekly meeting with a counselor to make sure that the contraceptive is being used regularly and properly. During these sessions, school, family, peer, and employment issues are also explored.

The young people in the program are urged to view the physicians as "their doctors." They can see the doctors and the nurse without an appointment and can discuss any health or related areas with them.

Mental Health

Mental Health Services. While working with young people and their families on education, health, employment, and support services, we frequently discover, or are told about, interpersonal problems, family discord, and other crises that are affecting their functioning. Often it is the presence of these problems that cause them to act impulsively, and/or to experience repeated failures in school, work, and peer relationships.

Professional social work services and counseling are offered, three days per week, by certified social workers. Because of the "family" quality of this program, referrals are usually made on an informal basis and frequently teens or their family will self-refer.

Combining the Best Efforts

Researchers have warned that teenage pregnancy is often the result of a congeries of interrelated factors: poverty, low self-esteem, and academic failure (or the sense that academic study is irrelevant). Effective programs combine the best efforts of schools, social service agencies, health-care providers, and other community groups. School-based programs have shown that they can prevent—or at least reduce the effects of—teen pregnancies.

Mary C. McClellan, *Phi Delta Kappan*, June 1987.

Clinical assessments are prepared on each individual who is seen for ongoing counseling and the more complex cases are referred to The Children's Aid Society's mental health unit.

Self-Esteem Enhancement Through the Performing Arts. This ongoing self-expression program, taught by professional actors and actresses from the National Black Theatre, is offered to both parents and teens. In weekly two-hour workshops, parents and teens explore issues, through music, dance, role-play, and dramatization which range from conflict resolution—in school and at home—to how to present oneself for a job interview. The sessions also offer a forum for discussing gender roles, family roles, affection, intimacy, culture, values, and racism. This medium enables the youngsters and adults to experiment with various scenarios and conclusions, and allows them to see themselves and their peers from new perspectives. In addition, these workshops provide opportunities for reflection, feedback, recognition, and applause.

Helping Kids Achieve

Lifetime Individual Sports. In this unusual program component, young people learn skills in lifetime sports such as squash, tennis, golf, and swimming. From a skills development standpoint, these activities are all "unforgiving sports" which require precise mastery and the exercise of self-discipline and self-control. We believe that the skills and the discipline learned in these sports—those that are necessary for having fun, for learning how to play with control, and for achieving success—are transferable to other aspects of the participants' everyday lives and can facilitate their learning to live with greater control over their lives. Moreover, it is our belief that the more opportunities young people have to consistently practice skills which require self-discipline and impulse control, the more likely it is that they will be able to exercise the restraint necessary for delaying early sexual activity. If they should decide to have intercourse, these types of experiences may also help them develop the discipline and control necessary for the consistent and correct use of contraceptives, so that unintended pregnancies can realistically be avoided.

Academic Assessment and Homework-Help Program. Each teen has a thorough academic assessment which is conducted by a team of specialists. Scores are obtained in math, reading, writing, and basic age-appropriate life concepts. After thorough testing, a "prescription" is developed for each teen, which summarizes his or her strengths and deficits and serves as a basis for ongoing individual and small group tutorials. Staff education experts, and a group of volunteers from the New York Junior League, use the academic prescriptions to provide one-on-one and/or small group educational support for the teens several days a week at regularly scheduled times at the Dunlevy Milbank Center.

Separate from the tutorial programs, we also provide a homework-help program, two afternoons a week, during which educators assist young people with homework assignments and/or school-related problems.

The Gannet Foundation funds the educational support structures that assist our young people from junior high school to college.

Job Club and Career Awareness Program. Through this weekly two-hour program, conducted by our employment specialists, young people explore the types of career possibilities available to them and learn, in concrete terms, about the world of work. To date, each youngster in this program has secured a social security card; has accurately completed working papers; and has learned

104

how to complete employment applications in an intelligent fashion. Moreover, they have taken part in several role-playing job interviews—appropriately dressing for each.

Each of the teens participating in this program must secure a part- or full-time summer position. Those who are twelve and thirteen—too young for working papers and typical part-time jobs—participate in our Entrepreneurial Apprenticeship Program. Through this program, they—and older teens who have chosen to be involved—work at various community functions (basketball games, dances, etc.) selling hot dogs, soda, juice and snacks. They earn a minimum hourly wage and participate—at the end of a specific period—in a modest profit-sharing program based on the degree to which they have fulfilled their job responsibilities.

The Example of Other Countries

A study that compared the U.S. with other developed western nations concluded that those countries with the most liberal attitudes toward sex, the most extensive sex education programs, and the most easily accessible contraceptive services had the *lowest* rates of teenage pregnancy, abortion, and childbearing.

Asta M. Kenney, *Phi Delta Kappan*, June 1987.

All the young people, who have participated in the employment program at our Central Harlem site in the Dunlevy Milbank Center, have opened bank accounts at the Carver Federal Savings Bank at 125th Street in Harlem. They are learning that banks, like college, are a reasonable expectation in their future. In addition, they are learning about interest rates and how to save and spend in a controlled, systematic way. In this unique program component, thrift, self-sufficiency, and planning are emphasized.

A College Education

College Admission Program. As far as we know, this is the only program of its kind that has received a commitment from a college president of a major university system. Donna Shalala, past president of Hunter College, convened a meeting of all the teens and parents in our program and presented them with certificates. These certificates guaranteed their acceptance, as fully matriculated freshmen in an accredited college (Hunter College), upon completion of high school, participation in our Teen Pregnancy Primary Prevention Program, and the recommendation of the teen pregnancy project director. This commitment should serve as a concrete incentive to those young people who are interested in furthering their education and should affirm the fact that college is part of their future.

Many of the families of the youngsters in our program receive public assistance. The cost of college, therefore, could still make it impossible for some of these youngsters to attend. To address this situation, major costs at Hunter College will be paid through the numerous aid plans ordinarily available to young people who qualify for financial aid and through The Children's Aid Society's special fund, which supports youngsters who have financial needs that go beyond those supported by federal and state aid plans. Some financial support for education will also be available for those young people who participate in other CAS programs. In addition, academic support services will be provided, as needed, through the SEEK [Search for Education, Evaluation, and Knowledge] program and through a variety of other academic help programs available to the students of Hunter College.

The Results Thus Far

After 36 months of operation, there are 175 young people (90 males, 85 females), ages 10-18, and 75 parents in the program.

• Only two females have become pregnant; and, to the best of our knowledge, only one male has caused a pregnancy.

• All the teens in the program are attending junior and senior high school; and approximately three-quarters of them are at grade level.

• There has been no reported alcohol or drug abuse.

• One hundred teens worked at part-time or full-time jobs last summer; 49 are currently working at part-time jobs after school and on weekends.

• Eighty-nine teens have bank accounts at the Carver Federal Savings Bank.

• Four teens and four parents have begun course work at Hunter College.

"Sex education classes are failing to give the American people what they are entitled to expect for their children, and what their children deserve."

Sex Education Does Not Reduce Teen Pregnancy

William J. Bennett

William J. Bennett was the US secretary of education from 1985 to 1988 under the Reagan administration. He was appointed the nation's drug czar by George Bush in 1989. In the following viewpoint, excerpted from a speech before the National School Boards Association, Bennett argues that sex education is not reducing teen pregnancies. Sex education fails, he maintains, because it does not teach that premarital sex is wrong.

As you read, consider the following questions:

1. What evidence does the author present that sex education is not reducing teen pregnancy?
2. According to Bennett, what is lacking in sex education courses?
3. What does the author believe is the real message behind current sex education programs?

William J. Bennett, "Sex and the Education of Our Children," *America*, February 14, 1987.

Sex education is much in the news. Many states and localities are considering proposals to implement or expand sex-education curricula. I understand the reasons why such proposals are under consideration. And indeed, polls suggest that a substantial majority of the American people favor sex education in the schools. I too tend to support the idea. It seems reasonable to the American people—and to me—for the schools to provide another opportunity for students to become both more knowledgeable and more thoughtful about this important area of life. To have such matters treated well by adults whom students and their parents trust would be a great improvement on the sex curriculum available on the street and on television.

For several years now, though, I have been looking at the actual form the idea of sex education assumes once it is in the classroom. Having surveyed samples of the literature available to the schools, and having gained a sense of the attitudes that pervade some of the literature, I must say this: I have my doubts. It is clear to me that some programs of sex education are not constructive. In fact, they may be just the opposite. In some places, some people, to be sure, are doing an admirable job. But in all too many places, sex education classes are failing to give the American people what they are entitled to expect for their children, and what their children deserve.

Doubtful Benefits

Seventy percent of all high-school seniors had taken sex education courses in 1985, up from 60 percent in 1976. Yet when we look at what is happening in the sexual lives of American students, we can only conclude that it is doubtful that much sex education is doing any good at all. The statistics by which we may measure how our children—how our boys and girls—are treating one another sexually are little short of staggering:

• More than one-half of America's young people have had sexual intercourse by the time they are 17.

• More than one million teen-age girls in the United States become pregnant each year. Of those who give birth, nearly half are not yet 18.

• Teen pregnancy rates are at or near an all-time high. A 25-percent decline in birth rates between 1970 and 1984 is due to a doubling of the abortion rate during that period. More than 400,000 teen-age girls now have abortions each year.

• Unwed teen-age births rose 200 percent between 1960 and 1980.

• Forty percent of today's 14-year-old girls will become pregnant by the time they are 19.

These numbers are, I believe, an irrefutable indictment of sex education's effectiveness in reducing teen-age sexual activity and

pregnancies. For these numbers have grown even as sex education has expanded. I do *not* suggest that sex education has *caused*
the increase in sexual activity among youth; but clearly it has not
prevented it. As Larry Cuban, professor of education at Stanford
University, has written: "Decade after decade . . . statistics have
demonstrated the ineffectiveness of such courses in reducing
sexual activity [and] teen-age pregnancy. . . . In the arsenal of
weapons to combat teen-age pregnancy, school-based programs
are but a bent arrow. However, bent arrows do offer the illusion
of action."

No Moral Guidance

Why do many sex-education courses offer merely the illusion
of action? When one examines the literature and materials
available to the schools, one often discovers in them a certain pervasive tone, a certain attitude. That attitude is this: Offer students
technical information, offer the facts, tell them they have choices
and tell them what the consequences of those choices could be,
but do no more. And there is the problem.

A Dangerous Myth

The myth is that "sex education" is a process of giving scientific
information to young people, as a way of stemming a rising tide
of teen-age pregnancy. But the cold fact is that teen-age pregnancy
was headed sharply downward before "sex education" programs
became entrenched in our schools—and has gone back up afterward, especially where such programs have been most pervasive.

Thomas Sowell, *The Washington Times*, May 17, 1988.

Let me give you a few examples. And let me say that these are
not "worst case" examples—that is, they are not examples of the
most controversial and provocative material used in some sex-
education courses. These are, rather, examples of approaches commonly used in many schools.

A curriculum guide for one of the largest school systems in the
country suggests strategies to "help students learn about their own
attitudes and behaviors and find new ways of dealing with problems." For example, students are given the following so-called
"problem situation," asked to "improvise dialogue" and "act it
out" and then discuss "how everyone felt about the interactions."

Susan and Jim are married. He becomes intoxicated and has sex
with his secretary. He contracts herpes, but fails to tell Susan.
What will happen in this situation? How would you react if you
were Susan and found out?

The so-called "expected outcome" of this exercise of "acting out"
and "interacting" is to get the student "to recognize sexually

transmitted diseases as a threat to the individual."

Another lesson presents a situation of an unmarried girl who has become pregnant. Various parties in her life recommend various courses of action—from marriage to adoption to abortion. Having described the situation, the teacher is then supposed to ask the following questions: Which solution do you like best? Why? Which solution do you like least? Why? What would you do if you were in this situation?

And the "expected outcome" of this exercise is "to identify alternative actions for an unintended pregnancy." Now we know what will likely happen in the classroom discussion of this lesson. Someone will opt for one course of action; others will raise their hands and argue for something else; more will speak; the teacher will listen to all opinions and that will be that. The teacher will move on, perhaps saying the discussion was good—that students should be talking about this, and that as long as they are talking about it, even if they do not arrive at a clear position, they are somehow being educated.

Do We Give Up?

Now the point I would like to make is that exercises like these deal with very complex, sensitive, personal, serious and often agitated situations—situations that involve human beings at their deepest levels. But the guiding pedagogical instruction to teachers in approaching all such "sensitive and personal issues" is this: "Where strong differences of opinion exist on what is right or wrong sexual behavior, objective, informed and dignified discussion of both sides of such questions should be encouraged." And that's it—no more. The curriculum guide is loaded with devices to help students "explore the options," "evaluate the choices involved," "identify alternative actions" and "examine their own values." It provides some facts for students, some definitions, some information, lots of "options"—but that's all.

What's wrong with this kind of teaching? First, it is a very odd kind of teaching—very odd because it does not teach. It does not teach because, while speaking to a very important aspect of human life, it displays a conscious aversion to making moral distinctions. Indeed, it insists on holding them in abeyance. The words of morality, of a rational, mature morality, seem to have been banished from this sort of sex education.

To do what is being done in these classes is tantamount to throwing up our hands and saying to our young people: "We give up. We give up on teaching right and wrong to you. Here, take these facts, take this information, and take your feelings, your options, and try to make the best decisions you can. But you're on your own. We can say no more." It is ironic that, in the part of our children's lives where they may most need adult guidance, and where indeed I believe they most want it, too often the young find instead an abdication of responsible moral authority.

Now I ask this: Do we or do we not think that sex for children is serious business, entailing serious consequences? If we do, then we need to be more than neutral about it in front of our children. When adults maintain a studiously value-neutral stance, the impression likely to be left is that, in the words of one 12th-grader: "No one says not to do it, and by default they're condoning it." And a sex-education curriculum that simply provides options, and condones by default, is not what the American people want—nor is it what our children deserve.

The Right Thing

It is not that the materials used in most of our schools are urging students to go out and have sexual intercourse. In fact, they give reasons why students might want to choose not to have intercourse, and they try to make students "comfortable" with that decision. Indeed, you sometimes get the feeling that, for these guides, being "comfortable" with one's decision, with exercising one's "option," is the sum and substance of the responsible life. Decisions aren't right or wrong, decisions simply make you comfortable or not. It is as though "comfort" alone had now become our moral compass. These materials are silent as to any other moral standards, any other standards of right and wrong, by which a student might reach a decision to refrain from sex and which would give him or her the inner resources to stick by it.

It seems to me, then, if this is how sex education goes, that we should not wonder at its failure to stem the rising incidence of teen-age sex, teen-age pregnancies, teen-age abortions and single teen-age parents. One developer of a sex-education curriculum recently said: "If you measure success in terms of reduction of teen pregnancy, I don't know if it has been successful. But in terms of orientation and preparation for students to comfortably incorporate sexuality into their lives, it has been helpful." There's that telltale "comfortable." But American parents expect more than that from their schools. Americans consistently say that they want our schools to provide reliable standards of right and wrong to guide students through life. In short, I think most Americans want to urge, not what might be the "comfortable" thing, but the right thing. Why are we so afraid to say what that is?

"Sex education without moral guidance is harmful."

Sex Education Should Focus on Morality

James M. Arata

James M. Arata has taught in public schools in the Cincinnati, Ohio area for more than eighteen years. In the following viewpoint, he criticizes the sex education programs of Planned Parenthood, one of the country's largest family planning organizations. Planned Parenthood's efforts to persuade teenagers to use contraceptives have not decreased teen pregnancies, he argues. The only way to solve this problem, Arata writes, is to teach teenagers that sex before marriage is immoral.

As you read, consider the following questions:

1. According to the author, what have been the results of Planned Parenthood's programs?
2. Why does Arata believe teenagers should not be allowed to make their own decisions regarding sex?
3. According to the author, how can America solve its teenage pregnancy problem?

James M. Arata, "The Dangerous Trends in Sex Education," *Blumenfeld Education Letter*, February 1988. Excerpted with the author's permission, (4587 Lakeland Drive, Batavia, Ohio 45103) from a much longer public statement.

In a 1953 presentation before a number of Planned Parenthood workers, Dr. Lena Levine sounded a clarion call for American teenagers to help raise the curtain on a drama that came to be known as the "Sexual Revolution":

> Our alternative solution is to be ready as educators and parents to help young people obtain sex satisfaction before marriage. By sanctioning sex before marriage, we will prevent fear and guilt. We must also relieve those who have them of their fear and guilt feelings, and we must be ready to provide young boys and girls with the best contraception measures available so they will have the necessary means to achieve sexual satisfaction without having to risk possible pregnancy. We owe this to them.

Well, we have seen Dr. Levine's future, and it doesn't work. Fast forward to December, 1985: the House Select Committee on Children, Youth, and Families reports that there are now 1.1 million teenage pregnancies each year, of which 430,000 end in abortions. The controlling members of the committee decide that more sex education, more contraception, and introduction of so-called school-based health clinics are the solution. Planned Parenthood responds with a $1 million campaign to persuade the TV networks to lift their bans on contraceptive advertising.

Hold on there, don't call in the arsonists to put out the fire, says Rep. Dan Coats of Indiana in so many words as he presents the minority view on the Select Committee: "Progressively over the last 25 years we have, as a nation, decided that it is easier to give children pills than to teach them respect for sex and marriage. Today we are seeing the results not only in increased pregnancy rates but in increased rates of drug abuse, venereal disease, suicide, and other forms of self-destructive behavior," comments Mr. Coats.

Planned Parenthood's Failure

Approximately 10% of the unwed 15- to 19- year-old girls in our country now become pregnant—about twenty times the rate when Planned Parenthood was officially founded in 1942. Almost half of those young girls will abort their babies, often at their friendly neighborhood Planned Parenthood clinic. Caring for the illegitimate children who haven't been suffocated, poisoned, pickled, or dismembered by the abortionist now costs the country an estimated $17 billion a year, a 600% increase in the last 20 years.

Even Planned Parenthood has had to admit failure. The September/October 1980 issue of *Family Planning Perspectives*, published by Planned Parenthood's research arm, the Alan Guttmacher Institute, stated that "More teenagers are using contraceptives and using them more consistently than ever before. Yet the number and rate of premarital pregnancies continues to rise." Six years later, the same publication stated that 18.4% of the young women who had relied on condoms to prevent pregnancy had in fact become pregnant.

A study by Dr. Dinah Richard, entitled "Teenage Pregnancy and Sex Education in the Schools—What Works and What Does Not Work," reaches an important summary conclusion on the issues of teenage pregnancy and venereal disease: *sex education without moral guidance is harmful*—both for kids and for society at large.

Contraception Hasn't Helped

Dr. Richard is particularly critical of scholastic sex-ed programs and public agencies which promote a false sense of security among adolescents by sanctioning their use of contraceptives. She points out that although federal expenditures on so-called "family planning" and "pregnancy prevention" programs *quadrupled* from 1971 to 1981, there was a 48% increase in teenage pregnancies (to 1.1 million a year) and a 133% increase in the abortion rate for girls aged 15 to 19 during the same decade. She also mentions America's epidemic of venereal disease—which involves 20 million cases of venereal herpes, 5 million cases of chlamydia, and thousands of people dying of AIDS.

Teach Abstinence, Not Promiscuity

The time has come for the American public to demand that the public schools teach children to say NO to fornication. . . .

There simply isn't any "safe" sex for schoolchildren. Courses and teachers that instruct otherwise are betraying the confidence that parents and the public have put in them in entrusting children to their care. Schoolchildren should be taught to practice abstinence until marriage and fidelity after marriage, and to expect your future spouse to do likewise.

Phyllis Schlafly, *The Phyllis Schlafly Report*, February 1987.

Dr. Richard arrives at her conclusions through analysis of a large number of separate research studies. These investigations provide grounds for a general indictment of both teenage contraceptive programs and the sex-education curricula that are currently found in most schools. Here are some of the topical statements drawn from these separate reports.

1. Though the teenage pregnancy rate jumped from the 1960's to the 1970's, the pregnancy rate has remained fairly steady through the 1980's. The birth rate for teens has dropped, however, due to an "epidemic" of abortions.

2. A sizeable percentage (28%) of teenage pregnancies are intended rather than accidental.

3. Federal funding for family-planning programs has increased, not decreased, the problem of teenage pregnancy.

4. Regular use of . . . contraceptives has not reduced teenage pregnancies.

5. Contraceptives have not decreased teen abortions.

6. Contraceptive education increases teen promiscuity.

7. Modern sex education ignores the principles of developmental psychology with regard to children and teenagers, thereby creating psychological problems in young people. In particular, modern sex educators tend to ignore the latency period in child development.

8. Modern sex education has not only created problems for youngsters, but has gone on to cause problems for the same people during their adulthood.

9. Modern sex education often fails to teach young people about the physically and psychologically harmful consequences of contraception and abortion, or the signficant likelihood of developing sexually transmitted diseases (STD's) and cervical cancer.

10. And once again, Dr. Richard's summary conclusion: Sex education is not beneficial without moral instruction. . . .

Children Don't Think

We seem to have a fascination with allowing kids to make premature *choices* in the realm of human sexuality. Adults generally don't allow immature children to make choices in such aspects of their daily lives as nutrition, proper rest, toilet training, school attendance. . . . So why do so many sex-education (and for that matter, so many "drug-education") programs presume mature decision-making capability on the part of children?

I presently teach mathematics to three sections of 8th graders. I find that a number of these children cannot even take sufficient initiative to bring their books, their homework, their pen and pencil to class. I *train* such children to assume proper minimal degrees of responsibility. I don't give them choices in the matter, because their failure to assume personal responsibility will eventually have serious consequences for both themselves and the society which might have to support them. Isn't that also the case with teenage pregnancy and venereal disease (and drug involvement)?

Let's remember that children don't think like adults. When we as adults discuss sexual matters, we can think in the symbolic and the abstract. But when children deal with such things, they operate in the concrete: words trigger pictures; pictures trigger action (experimentation).

So let's not subject our kids to the de-sensitizing (modesty-removing) and de-moralizing exercises which have been inserted into school curricula nationwide by Planned Parenthood types.

115

Kindergartners don't really need to make coed visits to inspect toilets and urinals, followed by discussions of both slang words and proper terminology for anatomical features of males and females. And high schoolers really don't need to study illustrated guides for condom use and other "safe sex" practices. . . .

Teaching Values

One of the first questions we must ask ourselves, no matter what our economic background, is what have we done to teach our kids about the beauty and goodness of sex within a loving marriage.

Many will argue that most teens acquire an excellent education on sex through their schools. The major problem with many of our sex-education curriculums today is that they are not teaching values. We are often teaching our children about sex, but not when to have it, or with whom, or, more important, why.

James R. Kelly, *The Times-Picayune*, November 13, 1987.

Given the dimensions of America's problem with teenage pregnancy and venereal disease, and given the patent failure of programs currently in place to deal with those problems, I suggest consideration of several common-sense ideas:

1. We must define what we mean by "sex education," and *clearly establish its strategic purpose in our schools.* At one end of the spectrum, as pointed out by a newsletter I once heard quoted, are the Ten Commandments and all that they imply. At the other end of the spectrum is a pimp teaching a young girl how to be a prostitute. The end toward which we should gravitate seems obvious.

The Answer Is No

Ted Koppel, ABC's "Nightline" host, had the right idea in the graduation address he gave at Duke in 1987: "We have actually convinced ourselves that slogans will save us. 'Shoot up if you must, but use a clean needle.' 'Enjoy sex whenever and with whomever you wish, but wear a condom.' No! That answer is no. Not because it isn't cool or smart or because you might end up in jail or dying in an AIDS ward, but no because it's wrong, because we have spent 5000 years as a race of rational human beings, trying to drag ourselves out of the primeval slime by searching for truth and moral absolutes. In its purest form, truth is not a polite tap on the shoulder. It is a howling reproach. What Moses brought down from Mount Sinai were not the Ten Suggestions."

If the mission of the program includes prevention of teenage pregnancy and reduction in the frequency of venereal disease infections, then it would appear that adoption of the K-12 programs currently being promoted throughout the country is ill-advised. These programs serve to entrench much of what has failed already.

2. We should hold back on sex education until the subject is developmentally appropriate for the child. We should then insure that the instruction provided is firmly grounded in traditional moral principles and traditional family ideals—not Planned Parenthood chic.

3. Parents and teachers must do a better job of educating children about the importance of postponing sexual involvement until after marriage. Marriage should be presented as the most moral, most fulfilling, and most societally beneficial situation in which sexual involvement can be experienced. Promotion of the contraceptive mentality compromises that message. Perhaps what we really need is *parent education*.

4. If we must teach sex education, then a positive, pro-active approach to sex education, such as Coleen Mast's Sex Respect program, should be adopted. Sex Respect promotes chastity as a healthy, cost-effective alternative to the popular contraceptive mentality. In other words, children should be taught firmly that is the only 100% reliable method of birth control and venereal disease protection. Again, teaching about contraceptives compromises that message.

5. We should ensure that materials which unnecessarily contradict the message of abstinence are removed from school libraries and resource centers. Specifically, magazines like *Ms.*, which runs articles like "Multiorgasmic Men," "Teen Lust," and "Gay Gothic," and ads for "sexual aids," witchcraft, and lesbianism, should be removed.

Choosing Who Speaks

6. We should realize that sex education is as much a matter of style as of substance. Who teaches is as important as what is being taught.

7. We should avoid values-neutral education which unwisely tells immature children that they have a wide range of choices.

8. We should separate the sexes for any sex education program that is contemplated. Youngsters who come into the classroom with natural modesty should be permitted to retain it.

9. We should exercise great care before inviting outside speakers to tell students about sexual issues. Otherwise, we may wind up with another Walter Sherman (President of AIDS Volunteers of Cincinnati), who not only plied a student audience with misinformation but went on to suggest that if the girls in the audience were to carry condoms in their purses, they could easily cover their heads in a rainstorm . . . and if a condom could cover their heads, well then, a condom could easily cover his fist . . . and if a condom could easily cover his fist, well then. . . . Walter, who

is nominally an Episcopalian minister, also told a young woman after his talk that the Bible is deficient in that it "just says *no.*"

10. We must observe the legal requirements of the Hatch amendment and its attendant enforcement regulations.

11. We must utilize our collective power to require that our legislators and governmental agencies stop subsidizing both promiscuity and illegitimate births with massive government funding. Simple economics tells us that what we subsidize, we promote.

12. We must work cooperatively to change the glamorization of sex that occurs on TV, on records, and in the print media.

13. To the extent possible, we should base decisions in the realm of sex education on hard facts rather than speculative opinion.

In the final analysis, as Betty Kuehner said in an editorial letter, "There is only one thing that must be given to children who want to be sexually active, and that is how to say 'NO.'" And those children who don't care about sexual activity should not be energized by school programs to give it a try.

"Our society . . . has chosen to repress teenage sexuality even at the risk of encouraging pregnancy."

Sex Education Should Not Focus on Morality

Faye Wattleton

Faye Wattleton is president of Planned Parenthood Federation of America, one of America's largest family planning organizations. It provides information on contraception, abortion, sterilization, and infertility. It is well known for its stance in favor of sex education. In the following viewpoint, Wattleton explains that such education should teach teenagers to be responsible without denigrating sexuality. She objects to imposing the moral standards of one segment of society on all teenagers.

As you read, consider the following questions:

1. According to Wattleton, what should guide efforts to reduce teenage pregnancies?
2. Why does Wattleton object to the government's moral agenda?
3. According to the author, how can the problem of teenage pregnancy be solved?

Faye Wattleton, "Coming of Age: The Tragedy of Teenage Pregnancy." Reprinted from USA Today Magazine, January 1989. Copyright 1989 by the Society for the Advancement of Education.

Teenage pregnancy is one of the most tragic phenomena our country faces. It is a tragedy whose high costs are unacceptable for the young people and their families who must bear the anguish and for all of us as a nation, since the economic burden often falls on society. Reducing the rate of teenage pregnancy in this country should be a high priority, and our efforts should be guided by compassion and common sense.

We must display compassion for the more than 1,000,000 teenagers who become pregnant each year—500,000 of whom will give birth, while 400,000 will choose to have an abortion and 100,000 will miscarry. Many of these young women and their children face a permanently diminished future. Teenage pregnancy lies at the very heart of blighted hopes, closed opportunities, and the vicious cycle of poverty.

Almost 12,000,000 teenagers are sexually active. Most engage in sexual activity almost a full year before they visit a family planning clinic, do not use contraceptives, or do not use them consistently.

The Consequences

The health consequences are overwhelming. The younger the mother, the more likely it is that she will suffer from complications of pregnancy and premature delivery. Compared to an older woman, she is twice as likely to die in childbirth, and her child is twice as likely to die before its first birthday. Even if the young mother and her child survive, they often face a future of despair. Teenage mothers often never finish high school, are three times more vulnerable to separation or divorce than women who delay childbearing, and have more unintended children during their lifetime. Not surprisingly, this results in a direct correlation between teenage pregnancy and poverty. Without an education and without a male partner, teenage mothers and their children are seven times more probable to be poor. Worst of all, the tragedy is compounded with each new generation—the younger the mother, the more likely she had a teenage parent.

Even if we were not concerned with the health and well-being of America's young, our society must worry about the teenage pregnancy problem for purely selfish reasons. Government-funded health and welfare programs for families started by teenage mothers cost almost $17,000,000,000 a year.

The media attention to this problem has been prominent, but limited, and focused almost entirely on the black community. Yet, an interstate analysis of teen pregnancy in the U.S., published in *Family Planning Perspectives*, showed that race is relatively unimportant in teenage fertility. The primary factors include poverty, urbanization, family stress, and crime—in short, the broad social setting in which teens make or don't make decisions about sexuality and reproduction. Thus, teenage pregnancy and child-bearing disproportionately affect blacks because they are more likely to be poor and disenfranchised. However, disadvantaged white teenagers also are threatened. In fact, the birth rate among black teens is leveling off, while the rate among white teens continues unabated. We must care about all of these young people as deeply and compassionately as we care for our own children, because they *are* our children.

Common Sense

We also must be guided by plain, old-fashioned common sense. Other Western nations certainly have a lot more of it than we do. Their rates of teenage pregnancy are far lower than ours because they recognize sexual development as a normal part of human development. Our society, however, has chosen to repress teenage sexuality even at the risk of encouraging pregnancy. We fail miserably in preparing our children to cope with the often inaccurate sexual messages they confront on a daily basis. We should

© Rosen/Rothco

121

ask ourselves the following questions: Is it rational to accept pregnancy as a just punishment for unacceptable sexual conduct? Is pregnancy the price our young people should pay for being bombarded with sexual messages in the media that say "do it" everywhere they turn? Is it the price they must pay for our inability to guide them to sexual maturation—a fact of life that can not be halted? Are we willing to sacrifice the lives of our children to continue policies that are intolerant of anything but sexual abstinence? Have we given our young people the best possible options for making decisions, or have we abdicated our responsibility as a society by ignoring the problem, rather than solving it? Are we more concerned about satisfying our moral standards than we are about protecting our children? . . .

Sensible Solutions

It is common sense to focus on primary prevention, even though, in America these days, many programs are designed to help teenagers become better parents. It is common sense for parents to talk with their children about sexuality—early, openly, and consistently. Such communication between parent and child not only delays the age of first intercourse, it also increases the likelihood that teenagers will use contraceptives when they do become sexually active. Parents are aware of their responsibility in this area. Yet, a 1985 Planned Parenthood/Louis Harris poll found that only one-third of American parents had discussed contraception with their children.

Since many parents still are unable to deal with their own sexuality, much less their children's, it is also sensible to encourage sexuality education in every school district in the country, from kindergarten through 12th grade. Only five states and the District of Columbia currently mandate sexual education, and only 10% of adolescents, and an even lower percentage of younger children, receive timely, comprehensive sexuality education in U.S. school systems. Denying children accurate information only leaves them open to misinformation and exploitation.

Finally, it would be reasonable for television network officials to present more balanced and responsible information about sex on television. This position is supported by 78% of Americans, according to our 1985 poll, and by the National Research Council, a Congressionally chartered organization that is the working arm of the National Academy of Sciences (official advisor to the Federal government on scientific and technical matters). A 1987 poll conducted for Planned Parenthood by Louis Harris and Associates showed that many young people actually believe what they see on television. They learn the facts of life from Alexis Carrington ("Dynasty") and J.R. Ewing ("Dallas"). However, when did Alexis or J.R. ever mention contraception? Birth control has become an accepted part of American life, yet television network officials still claim it is controversial; they accept ads for insecticides called "birth control for roaches," but ban birth control ads for people.

The European Example

Just as counterproductive are those who would restrict access to contraceptives for sexually active teens. European societies with significantly lower rates of teen pregnancy make contraceptives widely available in drugstores, supermarkets, vending machines, and in school-linked health clinics. However, there is a great controversy over these clinics in this country. A study of school-linked clinics in Baltimore showed that providing knowledge and contraceptive services does not increase sexual acitivity—in fact, it results in postponement of first sexual intercourse and in fewer pregnancies.

Making Decisions Themselves

One argument is that sex education doesn't teach "traditional" moral values. But the problem always gets to be, whose values are you going to teach? The major religious faiths don't agree on sexual ethics. You can't go into the classroom and teach children that premarital sex is okay: a lot of parents strongly disagree. You can't teach that it's always wrong either: a lot of the younger parents lived together before they were married and see little wrong in it. What you have to do is help young people find ways to make intelligent decisions for themselves.

James Collier, *Reader's Digest,* May 1981.

In the U.S., we see continual attacks not only against confidential family planning services for teens, but also against our national family planning program, funded through Title X of the Public Health Service Act. This program is the primary source of contraception for teens and poor women, and saves two to three dollars for every dollar spent. As a society, we must eliminate all financial barriers to contraception for teens, another position supported by the National Research Council.

Fixing the System

The scope of America's teenage problem requires a national commitment, but a Congressional report tells us that such a commitment does not exist. In 1986, the Select Committee on Children, Youth, and Families reported: "There is no focused approach to solving the complex problems of teen pregnancy at any level of government. The efforts that do exist are too few, uncoordinated, and lack significant support. In short, the system is broken."

Fortunately, there are ways to fix that broken system, and they are supported by the vast majority of Americans. According to our poll, 67% favor laws that would require public schools to establish links with family planning clinics; 85% want sexuality education programs offered in schools; and 78% would like birth control messages on television programs, in advertising, and in public service announcements.

There is no doubt that most of us favor knowledge over ignorance, common sense over moralistic rhetoric, and compassion over punishment. The challenge is to ensure that public opinion is translated into concrete efforts, that preventing teenage pregnancy becomes part of our national agenda, and that, for future generations, the coming of age in America will be accompanied by the right and means to become an adult before becoming a parent.

Distinguishing Bias from Reason

When dealing with controversial issues, many people allow their feelings to dominate their powers of reason. Thus, one of the most important critical thinking skills is the ability to distinguish between statements based upon emotion or bias and conclusions based upon a rational consideration of the facts.

The following statements are taken from the viewpoints in this chapter. Consider each statement carefully. *Mark R for any statement you believe is based on reason or a rational consideration of the facts. Mark B for any statement you believe is based on bias, prejudice, or emotion. Mark I for any statement you think is impossible to judge.*

If you are doing this activity as a member of a class or group, compare your answers with those of other class or group members. Be able to defend your answers. You may discover that others come to different conclusions than you do. Listening to the rationale others present for their answers may give you valuable insights in distinguishing between bias and reason.

> R = *a statement based upon reason*
> B = *a statement based on bias*
> I = *a statement impossible to judge*

1. Sex education programs make children more self-confident. If they have self-confidence, they will be able to say no when pressured to have sex.

2. Nature never intended for children to go to school to learn how to mate.

3. Sex is not like reading or writing or other skills that need to be taught. Thus sex education is completely unnecessary.

4. Homosexuality has become popular in the wake of the growth of sex education. This is because sex education programs state that homosexuals should be invited into the classroom and allowed to describe homosexual practices in detail.

5. Adults generally don't allow immature children to make choices in such aspects of their daily lives as nutrition, proper rest, or school attendance. They should not be allowed to make their own decisions about sex, either.

6. Often parents don't discuss explicit sexual issues, such as homosexuality and masturbation, because they are too embarrassed. Trained sex educators are better able to deal with these issues.

7. Asking sex educators to reduce teen pregnancy is like calling in the arsonists to put out the fire.

8. When you start talking publicly about sex you are intruding on the private sex life of individuals, which is unnatural.

9. Children don't think like adults. Adults can think abstractly, but children only think in the concrete.

10. European societies with significantly lower birth rates than the US make contraceptives widely available in drugstores, supermarkets, and vending machines.

11. Sex education has not decreased the teen pregnancy rate.

12. Teenage mothers rarely finish high school. Without an education, they are seven times more probable to be poor than adult mothers.

13. Teenagers are not merely overgrown children.

14. Television glamorizes sex.

15. Pregnancy is just punishment for teenagers' immoral sexual behavior.

Periodical Bibliography

The following articles have been selected to supplement the diverse views presented in this chapter.

America	"Advising Teen-Agers To Say No," April 23, 1988.
Mary Cartledge-Hayes	"A Mother's Day Challenge," *Ms.*, May 1987.
Midge Decter	"Sex Education on Trial," *Crisis*, December 1988.
Mitch Finley	"Parents Should Teach the Joy of Sex," *U.S. Catholic*, February 1989.
Erica Goode	"Telling '80s Kids About Sex," *U.S. News & World Report*, November 16, 1987.
Joyce A. Little	"The Gender Gap," *Crisis*, January 1989.
David McAllister	"Assessing the Health of Sex Education in a Time of Dis-Ease," *SIECUS Report*, September/October 1988. Available from SIECUS, 32 Washington Place, New York, NY 10003.
Elizabeth Marek	"The Lives of Teenage Mothers," *Harper's Magazine*, April 1989.
Connaught C. Marshner	"The Growth of Sex Respect," *Conservative Digest*, December 1988.
Massachusetts Bishops	"Sex Education: Information or Formation?" *Origins*, December 31, 1987. Available from the National Catholic News Service, 1312 Massachusetts Ave. NW, Washington, DC 20005.
New York Woman	"Teens Talk About Sex," March/April 1987.
William J. O'Malley	"Teen-Agers and . . . You Know What," *America*, April 15, 1989.
Parents	"The Subject Is Sex," August 1988.
Phyllis Schlafly	"The High Costs of Free Sex," *The Phyllis Schlafly Report*, February 1987. Available from The Eagle Trust Fund, Box 618, Alton, IL 62002.
Lindsy Van Gelder and Pam Brandt	"Beyond Sex Ed," *McCall's*, May 1987.

127

Is Pornography Harmful?

SEXUAL
VALUES

Chapter Preface

A central question related to pornography is whether viewing pornographic material that combines sex and violence causes men to reenact this violence.

For example, Ted Bundy, who was sentenced to the electric chair and executed for raping and murdering a twelve-year-old girl, claimed he was influenced by pornography. Later Bundy confessed to the murders of twenty-three women; investigators speculate that the number may have been closer to fifty. According to Bundy, pornography can be addictive and fuel a fantasy life that can be satisfied only by committing violence. Researcher Edward Donnerstein has also concluded that pornography increases men's aggressiveness toward women. Donnerstein and his colleague, Neil Malamuth, exposed college-age men to hours of pornographic films. After this exposure, two-thirds of the men claimed that they would force a woman into sex acts if they were convinced they would not be caught or punished.

Critics like psychologist Donald Mosher, on the other hand, contend that the effects of pornography are unclear. Mosher argues that no study has shown conclusively that pornography causes violence against women. Mosher says that studies such as Donnerstein's have been contradicted by other studies, and therefore cannot be considered reliable. Other researchers cite Denmark as proof that pornography is not harmful: Since pornography's legalization there in 1967 the number of sex crimes has dropped.

The authors in the following chapter debate whether pornography causes women to become victims of sexual violence.

129

"Women . . . are harmed by the practice of pornography."

Pornography Is Harmful

Susan G. Cole

Susan G. Cole is a Canadian journalist who has written extensively on pornography. In the following viewpoint, excerpted from a speech, Cole argues that all forms of pornography, whether violent or not, are harmful. Cole writes that women are often coerced or forced into making pornography. She also believes that pornography degrades women by presenting them as sex objects.

As you read, consider the following questions:

1. Why does the author mistrust nonviolent pornography?
2. According to Cole, how does pornography affect the way men treat women?
3. Why is Cole opposed to obscenity laws?

Susan G. Cole, "Pornography: What Do We Want?" in *Good Girls/Bad Girls*, edited by Laurie Bell. Toronto, Ontario: The Women's Press, 1987. Reprinted with permission.

Often women are coerced and forced into performing for pornography. This I refer to as *sexual subordination*. My definition of pornography is the practice of presenting sexual subordination for sexual gratification. That's how I see it. This is a tool for analysis to figure out whether pornography is happening.

I want to unpack some of the aspects of this practice. First the conditions under which these things are made. I noticed, for example, that the pictures really weren't going to tell the whole story because people had been looking at pictures of women being brutalized and not noticing that there might be some harm there. Instead we have judges saying, "One man's this is another man's that." Or our own customs agent, who, when asked how he didn't notice that *Penthouse* in December of 1984 was distributing photographs of women being tightly bound, hanging from trees and pegs and rocks, said, "Well, the violence is only implied."

I realized that the pictures aren't going to help us because pornography has been so successful that we're not even real people anymore—we're only things. People don't even notice that anything's going on in the material where a woman is being harmed, let alone where there is the appearance of consensual sex going on. Women are being brutalized whether the gun is in the camera frame or not.

Fact, Not Fantasy

Next, looking at the picture, I note that it is there to turn somebody on. The pictures are supposed to be doing something. This is not a fantasy. Neither is it an idea. This may not apply to lesbians, but the next time any of you apprehend an erection, either your own or somebody else's, look at it very carefully and tell me that it's a fantasy. Tell me it's an idea, and if it is speech, what is it saying?

Now I want to address the issues surrounding the consumption of this material. I could sit and quote you clinical studies from all kinds of people who have been doing work in laboratory settings, but I will not. Some of this work is valuable because it's being done by men, and so people believe them. But I don't need some man to sit in a laboratory and tell me that rape is happening.

I've been talking to women and asking them what they think about pornography and what pornography has meant in their lives. I have been talking to a particular group of women, admittedly—I have been surveying shelters for assaulted women. I ask, "What does the word *pornography* mean to you?" They talk about being terrorized. They talk about men saying, "Look at that. Why can't you do that? Replicate that." The men don't know that Linda Lovelace [in the movie *Deep Throat*] did that because she was forced to do it and not every woman wants to do it. When these women tell me what is happening to them, I believe them. And if we don't believe them, nobody else will.

Sometimes the pictures are pretty clear about what they are doing to sexuality. They are making sexuality look pretty much one-dimensional, that is, men on top, women on the bottom—period. You see the hierarchy, the violence, and the definition of *male* fused with dominance and the definition of *female* fused with submission. They are making inequality sexy. Not only are they making inequality sexy, they are making it sexual.

Objectifying Men

Consider how difficult it has been to reverse the situation. Bob Guccione and the *Penthouse* empire tried to sell beefcake to women the way he sold cheesecake to men. He produced a magazine called *Viva* in 1972. It featured sexually explicit accounts of women's sexual adventures punctuated with male nudes. The problem was where to display it. Put it beside *Playboy* and *Penthouse*, and he doesn't get his targetted audience. Put it beside *Chatelaine* and *Good Housekeeping*, and he causes apoplexy among the readers of those magazines.

Destroyed Relationships

Pornography constitutes a direct attack on significant relationships because it helps create a mind-set that eventually treats all people as sexual objects. Modern pornography is an education system. It teaches. Its message is: Human beings are mere animals; the highest value is immediate pleasure; other people may be used and abused and then discarded. It teaches that sex is divorced from love, commitment, morality, and responsibility, that perversion is to be preferred to normality, that women are fair game for anyone who cares to exploit them.

The Arthur S. DeMoss Foundation, *The Rebirth of America*, 1986.

But eventually he did find his audience. Women were delighted. They used to have to settle for *Cosmopolitan* telling them how to land Mr. Right. Now they found out what happened once he was in hand, and they liked it. But they started to complain. They said, "These guys look gay." The producers of *Penthouse* did everything they could to make sure that this would not happen. They knew that if you spread a woman's legs and put her looking at a camera, she'll look sexy. But you can't do it with men. So they tried everything. They had him in forest settings. They had him looking out into the distance to make him look like he had control over the whole environment. They had him on horses so that he could look like the Marlboro man. And they still looked gay. This is not to cast aspersions on my gay brothers, but rather to say that when women looked at these pictures, they did not see what they considered masculine by conventional standards. My point is that if you reduce a woman to tits and ass, she'll look like a woman, but reduce a man, and he will not look masculine according to our standards.

When sexual abuse is eroticized and distributed to the tune of $8 billion dollars a year on this continent, with more outlets than there are McDonald's, this makes women feel like we're second-class citizens. We wonder: if this goes on as entertainment, how are we being viewed in society? The fact that people can look at the pictures and not see women getting hurt is even more of a problem.

Racism is being sexualized just as inequality is being sexualized. The image of Black women in pornography is almost consistently one featuring them breaking from chains. The image of Asian women in pornography is almost consistently one of being tortured. The best way to institutionalize a dynamic of power is to eroticize it.

The Problem with Laws

Obscenity laws are a problem for us, and I think we have to oppose them. Obscenity laws do two things. First of all, they rely on community standards, which in a sexist and heterosexist society are bound to be sexist and homophobic. It's no wonder that so much gay material comes under fire. My problem with community standards is that they suggest, as Catharine MacKinnon has said, that the problem with the pornographer is that he has chosen the wrong audience. If he could only find one that put up with women being hung up on meat hooks, everything would be just fine. . . .

Eroticizing Equality

The question is, what do we want? Here's what I want. I want a legal remedy that will give relief to women who are harmed by the practice of pornography. I want a legal remedy that's going to stop looking at the pictures, stop calling them fantasy, stop calling them representations and images and depictions and start viewing them as documents, presentations, and the reality of women and men in this culture. If men look carefully enough at the pictures, they may notice that pornography makes male sexuality look like that of a rapist, and they should be upset about it. I want a legal remedy that's going to redress harms. This is why I'm sympathetic to the . . . approach which defines pornography as a violation of women's civil rights. When men look at pornography, they see tits and ass. That's all. That isn't to say that our sex is bad, but we are more than that. It's important to expand the issue from "Oh, it's just about sexuality" and understand how all of this is affecting all of our lives everywhere.

I would really like to see as much time as is spent eroticizing inequality and hierarchy and dominance and power and violence and brutality spent on eroticizing equality. I don't even think we know what it would look like! And my greatest fear is that if we looked at it, we wouldn't even be turned on by it anymore.

"Emotional [arguments] against pornography . . . are false and, indeed, potentially very harmful."

Pornography Is Not Harmful

F.M. Christensen, interviewed by *Playboy*

In the following viewpoint, *Playboy*, a monthly magazine that features pornography, interviews Canadian philosopher F.M. Christensen. Christensen argues that pornography is a natural, positive way for people to satisfy their sexual desires. He believes that many women who oppose pornography are inhibited and ashamed of their own sexuality.

As you read, consider the following questions:

1. Why does Christensen contend that pornography is not dehumanizing?
2. What does Christensen believe to be the reason behind women's anger at pornography?
3. How does the author answer the charge that pornography promotes rape?

How many times have you sat through an antiporn diatribe or listened to a fundamentalist rail against erotica and wondered, Who will stand up for pornography? We asked Canadian philosopher Dr. F.M. Christensen to respond to some of the clichéd antiporn arguments.

PLAYBOY: Is pornography a recent phenomenon?

CHRISTENSEN: Humans have produced pornography for thousands of years. The artists of ancient Greece, India and Japan produced quite a bit of sexually explicit art. In ancient Tahiti, family entertainment included the portrayal of a variety of sex acts, and ancient Polynesians held nude beauty contests. In most early societies, evidently pornography was not considered disgusting or degrading.

PLAYBOY: Why do we have pornography?

CHRISTENSEN: Pornography is something like theater or spectator sports. Humans can get enjoyment by watching others because we have the ability to fantasize. In particular, we fantasize about sex; in fact, it's so natural that we even fantasize in our sleep. Pornography is a simple extension of sexual fantasy. It is an alternative way of satisfying, albeit imperfectly, some very strong needs and desires.

Fantasies Are Natural

PLAYBOY: But some people say that that makes pornography dehumanizing.

CHRISTENSEN: On the contrary, nothing is more human than sexual fantasies and feelings. If anyone is trying to dehumanize us, it is those who would denigrate our sexuality.

PLAYBOY: Does pornography turn people into sex objects?

CHRISTENSEN: Our long tradition of devaluing the body, and sex in particular, underlies this charge. An exercise video tape has just as much focus on the physical body—or the body as object—as does a pornographic movie. Why is sex object a common charge while exercise object is not?

PLAYBOY: Does pornography reduce people to body parts?

CHRISTENSEN: Look through almost any *non*erotic magazine and you will find advertisements and articles featuring hair, hands, hips, feet, etc. They may be selling foot powder or explaining how to keep hips in trim or how to reduce back pain. They are never condemned for reducing people to body parts. The real reason for the attack on pornography is that some people consider sex organs shameful.

A Limited View

PLAYBOY: Is pornography very narrow-minded? Does it present people as being nothing but sexual beings; does it carry the message that sex is all we're good for?

CHRISTENSEN: Most pornography has a limited scope; it contains little else besides sex. This is partly because sexual activity has been excluded from socially respectable portrayals of human experience; it has been driven out into a realm by itself. But almost all events, from sports to concerts, are specialized in their content. They all portray a limited view of human life. There are magazines that specialize in sports, food, music, hobbies, fashion, etc. Do these publications portray people as whole human beings? Do movies or novels that do *not* have sex scenes deny our completeness? No. Human wholeness in no way precludes focusing on one aspect of ourselves at a time.

Ed Gamble. Reprinted with permission.

You presume that pornography makes all women angry. This is not true. In fact, many of them enjoy sexually explicit presentation. Video dealers report that women and couples rent most X-rated movies. There are many women who *are* angered by pornography. However, the main reason for their anger stems from the bodily shame we've all been conditioned to feel. Those feelings are not healthy, and the best way to solve this problem is to educate people to be comfortable with their bodies. Another reason for women's anger is that they feel their careers have been restricted. In the past, they were largely limited to being sex partners and mothers and were not valued by society for their intelligence or creativity. Consequently, emphasis on a woman's desirability to men is seen as something bad in itself. The solution to this problem is not to eliminate attraction between the sexes but to continue to expand women's opportunities.

PLAYBOY: Do men's-magazines' images of women create an unreal standard of beauty?

CHRISTENSEN: The women pictured in, say, *Playboy* have faces and figures that the average woman can't match. Hence, comparison with them can only make a woman feel inferior and insecure. This is obviously not a legitimate objection to nudity itself. Should *Playboy* publish pictures of less attractive women? That wouldn't really satisfy those who object to pornography, for they don't make this same charge about idealization elsewhere in the media and the culture. For instance, children on television and in the movies are almost always cute and charming. The models in women's fashion magazines are certainly above average in attractiveness. How does an average man feel when he compares himself with most male movie stars? He certainly can't match their looks or status. But the real point here is that neither the media nor pornography creates the ideal of beauty. Every culture has its standard of physical attractiveness, and those who fall short feel inadequate. This problem will exist with or without pornography.

PLAYBOY: Is pornography male propaganda? It portrays women as being sexually assertive and uninhibited, and that is just not necessarily so.

CHRISTENSEN: In this respect, pornography is no different from any other fiction. It is *not* real life; its characters are idealized; they fulfill someone's fantasy. Does good always triumph over evil? Does true love always last forever? These are fantasies, too—not portrayals of real life. In fact, avoiding depicting sexuality in a work is more unrealistic, for it suggests that women and men are *non*sexual.

A Desire To Share Pleasure

PLAYBOY: Does pornography promote rape?

CHRISTENSEN: Some radical feminists make charges like that, but they are absurd when applied to nonviolent pornography. It's important to realize that these people make similar libelous claims about men and male sexuality in general. They say that all men are by nature violent. These extremists see antifemale messages everywhere. To them, sexual comments are never appreciative, only hostile. Similarly, then, they view pornography as another expression of men's desire to dominate women, not of their desire to have and share sexual pleasure.

Emotional reactions against pornography tell more about the complainant's own sexual inhibitions than about pornography. The fact is that these arguments are false and, indeed, potentially very harmful. Anyone who hears them should counter with the truth.

"Violent types of pornography . . . [were] an indispensable link in the chain of events that led to the behavior, the assaults, the murders."

Pornography Promotes Violence Against Women

Ted Bundy, interviewed by James Dobson

Ted Bundy was executed by the state of Florida for the murder of a twelve-year-old girl whom he abducted from a playground in 1978. He had confessed to murdering more than twenty-three women. In the following viewpoint, he discusses how pornography contributed to his violent behavior. He was interviewed by James Dobson, a psychologist with the religious radio program *Focus on the Family*.

As you read, consider the following questions:

1. What effect does pornography have on men, according to the author?
2. What was Bundy's purpose in granting this interview?
3. How would Bundy make society safer for women?

Dobson: Ted, it is about 2:30 in the afternoon. You are scheduled to be executed tomorrow morning at 7 o'clock, if you don't receive another stay. What is going through your mind? What thoughts have you had in these last few days?

Bundy: I won't kid you to say that it's something that I feel that I am in control of, or something that I have come to terms with, because I haven't. It is a moment by moment thing. Sometimes I feel very tranquil and other times I don't feel tranquil at all. What's going through my mind right now is to use the minutes and hours I have left as fruitfully as possible and see what happens. It helps to live in the moment in the essence that we use it productively. Right now I'm feeling calm in large part because I'm here with you.

Dobson: For the record, you are guilty of killing many women and girls. Is that correct?

Bundy: Yes. Yes, that's true.

Dobson: Ted, how did it happen? Take me back. What are the antecedents of the behavior that we've seen? So much grief, so much sorrow, so much pain for so many people. Where did it start, how did this moment come about?

Bundy: That's the question of the hour and one that not only people much more intelligent than I will be working on for years but one that I've been working on for years and trying to understand. Is there enough time to explain it all? I don't know. I think I understand it, though, what happened to me to the extent that I can see how certain feelings and ideas have developed in me, to the point that I began to act out certain very violent and very destructive feelings.

A Healthy Home

Dobson: Let's go back then to those roots. First of all, as I understand it, you were raised in what you considered to have been a healthy home. You were not physically abused, you were not sexually abused, you were not emotionally abused.

Bundy: No. No way. And that's part of the tragedy of this whole situation. Because I grew up in a wonderful home with two dedicated and loving parents, one of five brothers and sisters, a home where we as children were the focus of my parents' lives, where we regularly attended church, two Christian parents who did not drink, they did not smoke, there was no gambling, there was no physical abuse, or fighting in the home. I'm not saying this was "Leave It To Beaver."

Dobson: It wasn't a perfect home.

Bundy: No, I don't know if such a home exists, but it was a fine solid Christian home and I hope no one will try to take the easy way out and try to blame or otherwise accuse my family of contributing to this, because I know, and I'm trying to tell you as honestly as I know how, what happened. And I think this is the message I want to get across: that as a young boy, and I mean a boy of 12 or 13 certainly, that I encountered, outside the home again, in the local grocery store, in a local drug store, the soft-core pornography—what people call soft core. As young boys do, we explored the back roads and sideways and byways of our neighborhood, and often times people would dump the garbage and whatever they were cleaning out of their house. And from time to time, we would come across pornographic books of a harder nature than, of a more graphic, you might say, more explicit nature than we would encounter, let's say, in your local grocery store. And this also included such things as, let's say, detective magazines.

Dobson: Those that involved violence?

Bundy: Yes, yes, and this is something I think I want to emphasize is the most damaging kinds of pornography—and again I'm talking from personal experience—hard, real personal experience. Most damaging kinds of pornography are those that involve violence and sexual violence. Because the wedding of those two forces, as I know only too well, brings about behavior that is just, just too terrible to describe.

Wayne Stayskal. Reprinted by permission: Tribune Media Services.

Dobson: Now, walk me through that. What was going on in your mind at that time? What was happening?

Bundy: Before we go any further, I think it's important to me that people believe what I am saying. I tell you that I am not blaming pornography. I am not saying that it caused me to go out and do certain things. And I take full responsibility for whatever I have done and all the things I have done. That's not the question here.

The question and the issue is how this kind of literature contributed and helped mold and shape the kinds of violent behavior.

Dobson: It fueled your fantasies, didn't it?

Bundy: In the beginning it fuels this kind of thought process. Then at a certain time, it is instrumental in—I would say crystallizing—making into something which is almost like a separate entity inside. At that point, I was at the verge of acting out these kinds of thoughts.

Dobson: Now, I really want to understand that. You had gone about as far as you could go in your own fantasy life with printed material, or printed and video or film, magazine, what have you. And then there was the urge to take that little step, or big step over to a physical event?

Bundy: And it happened in stages, gradually. It didn't necessarily, not to me at least, happen overnight. My experience with pornography generally, but with pornography that deals on a violent level with sexuality, is once you become addicted to it—and I look at this as a kind of addiction like other kinds of addiction—I would keep looking for more potent, more explicit, more graphic kinds of material. Like an addiction, you keep craving something which is harder, harder, something which gives you a greater sense of excitement until you reach the point where the pornography only goes so far. You reach that jumping-off point where you begin to wonder if maybe actually doing it will give you that which is beyond just reading about it or looking at it.

I Couldn't Control It

Dobson: How long did you stay at that point before you actually assaulted someone?

Bundy: That is a very delicate point, by the way, in my own development. We're talking about having reached the point or gray area that, that surrounded that point over a course of years.

I would say a couple of years. And what I was dealing with there were very strong inhibitions against criminal behavior or violent behavior that had been conditioned into me, bred into me in my environment, in my neighborhood, in my church, in my school. Things that said, "No, this is wrong. Even to think of it is wrong, but certainly to do it is wrong." I'm on that edge, you might say the last vestiges of restraint, the barriers to actually doing

142

something were being tested constantly, and assailed through the kind of fantasy life that was fueled largely by pornography.

Dobson: Do you remember what pushed you over that edge? Do you remember the decision to go for it? Do you remember where you decided to throw caution to the wind?

Bundy: When you say pushed, I know what you're saying. I don't want to infer again that I was some helpless kind of victim. We're talking about an influence—that is, an influence of violent types of media, violent types of pornography—which was an indispensable link in the chain of events that led to the behavior, the assaults, the murders.

Porn Affects Everyone

Pornography affects the most dangerous sex-offender as well as the normal person, and it interferes with interpersonal relationships and personal moral development in *everyone* who uses it, not only the disturbed and demented. . . .

Normal, as well as disturbed people, not only become "desensitized" to soft-core materials, they also develop a fondness for more deviant materials. Both incorporate them into sexual practices, and begin to fantasize about, and even endorse, the use of force in their sexual relationships.

Dangerous offenders (i.e., child molesters, incest fathers, killers and rapists), develop a fondness for deviant material and incorporate it into their preparatory stimulation before seeking out a victim.

John Lofton, *The Washington Times*, February 1, 1989.

It's a very difficult thing to describe, the sensation of reaching that point where I knew that—it was like something had, say, snapped—that I knew that I couldn't control it any more, that these barriers that I had learned as a child, that had been instilled in me, were not enough to hold me back with respect to seeking out and harming somebody.

The Battle Within

Dobson: Would it be accurate to call that a frenzy, a sexual frenzy?

Bundy: Well, yes. That's one way to describe it, a compulsion—a building up of this destructive energy. Another factor here that I haven't mentioned is the use of alcohol. What alcohol did in conjunction with, let's say, my exposure to pornography was alcohol reduced my inhibitions at the same time the fantasy life that was fueled by pornography eroded them further.

Dobson: In the early days, you were nearly always about half-drunk when you did these things; is that right?

Bundy: Yes.

Dobson: Was that always true?

Bundy: I would say that was generally the case. Almost without exception.

Dobson: All right, if I can understand it now, there's this battle going on within. There are the conventions that you've been taught. There's the right and wrong that you learned as a child. And then there is this unbridled passion fueled by your plunge into hard-core, violent pornography. And those things are at war with each other.

Bundy: Yes.

Dobson: And then with the alcohol diminishing the inhibitions, you let go.

Bundy: Well, yes. And you can summarize it that way, and that's accurate, certainly. And it just occurred to me that some people would say that, well, I've seen that stuff, and it doesn't do anything to me. And I can understand that. Virtually everyone can be exposed to so-called pornography, and while they were aroused to it one degree or another, not go out and do anything wrong.

Dobson: Addictions are like that. They affect some people more than they affect others. . . .

Beyond Retribution

Dobson: Do you deserve the punishment the state has inflicted upon you?

Bundy: That's a very good question, and I'll answer it very honestly. I don't want to die, I'm not going to kid you. I kid you not. I deserve certainly the most extreme punishment society has, and I think society deserves to be protected from me and from others like me. That's for sure.

I think what I hope will come of our discussion is I think society deserves to be protected from itself. Because, as we've been talking, there are forces loose in this country, particularly against this kind of violent pornography where, on the one hand well-meaning decent people will condemn behavior of a Ted Bundy, while they're walking past a magazine rack full of the very kinds of things that send young kids down the road to be Ted Bundys. That's the irony.

We're talking here not just about morals. What I'm talking about is going beyond retribution, which is what people want with me; going beyond retribution and punishment because there is no way in the world that killing me is going to restore those beautiful children to their parents and correct and soothe the pain.

But I'll tell you there are lots of other kids playing in streets around this country today who are going to be dead tomorrow, and the next day and the next day and next month, because other young people are reading the kinds of things and seeing the kinds of things that are available in the media today.

"No one can show a causal relationship between exposure to porn and effects on behavior."

Pornography Does Not Promote Violence Against Women

Sol Gordon

Sol Gordon is a nationally known sex educator. He served as director of the Institute for Family Research and Education at Syracuse University in New York until his retirement in 1985. Since then, he has lectured across the country on sex education. In the following viewpoint, he suggests that factors other than pornography cause violence against women.

As you read, consider the following questions:

1. Why is the author against banning pornography?
2. What does Gordon suggest will stop violence against women?
3. Why does Gordon think the fight against pornography is dangerous?

Sol Gordon, "Pornography: A Humanist Issue." This article first appeared in *The Humanist* issue of July/August 1985 and is reprinted by permission.

145

The writer who is most frequently quoted in the area of pornography is Edward Donnerstein who said that there can be demonstrated a causal relationship between exposure to porn and effects on attitudes—especially college students, as they are very suggestible. But no one can show a causal relationship between exposure to porn and effects on behavior.

This issue is the most diversionary issue that we have in the feminist movement. I can tell you that the real issue is reproductive freedom, social justice, and sex education. Pornography is not a cause of anything. It is a symptom. It is a symptom, and we are playing games with this. Some of the best energy of the feminist movement is used to sleep in the same bed with the Moral Majority. It is no accident—you could not have gotten anywhere . . . without the active support of our worst enemies. It makes me angry. We need anger in this movement; we need drama in this movement. We are so quiet, so pleasant, and so nice—and that is why we are so ineffectual. If we could ban pornography tomorrow, in five years time I predict that there will be more rape, more sadomasochism, more child molestation than we have now. We have so little understanding of the fact that anything we ban we make more readily available. The wildest imagination leads us to believe that you can ban pornography. At the outset, I think I should say that I think those laws are an outrageous violation of civil liberties. You could use them to ban Erica Jong; you could ban the Bible. The Bible is one of the most masochistic, pornographic things we have in terms of humiliation of women. Women are supposed to be quiet in the Bible. If I was to talk about the real threat to women, I would talk about some of the influence of the Bible, some of the influence of prime-time television, the soaps, and advertising. Those are some of the much more serious threats than pornography.

Education, Not Prohibition

We need sex education. Every index of psychopathology, sexual pathology, is positively correlated with an uncomfortable, unhealthy attitude toward masturbation. Somehow or other we have socialized people, especially men, to think that it is much better to rape than to masturbate. We sent our people over to Vietnam, and we said to our young men, "You rape Vietnamese because rape is okay but not masturbation." Our young men can go off on a business trip, horny as hell. But they are married. They can't masturbate. They have to have sex—they have to rape somebody. And, of course, they come home to their wives, bringing flowers and venereal disease.

Haven't we learned the lesson that, if we ban pornography in Indianapolis, there will be a hundred places right around Indianapolis that would have all these things available? It would proliferate. Haven't we learned that lesson? And where do we get the nerve to sleep in the same bed with the Moral Majority and the Phyllis Schlaflys? Don't we get a little hint that there is something wrong with what we are doing? Why don't we put our energy into sex education? People who are into sex education find pornography boring. They are not interested; they are not involved in it. Haven't we learned anything from the Kinsey studies, in which they studied a thousand people who were imprisoned for sexually acting out and discovered that there was a far less degree of sexual involvement with pornography than there was in the outside general population? This is a diversionary issue! It is destroying and limiting the humanist movement, the feminist movement. We should get together and unite on real issues. The most important issue we are threatened with right now is reproductive freedom. We are going to lose the abortion issue. We are going to lose the abortion issue because some of the brightest, the most exciting elements of the feminist movement are concentrated on taking back the night. We need to take back the day!

Fighting the Eagle Forum

There is absolutely no evidence of a causal relationship between pornography and sexual acting out. I haven't seen it in sexual molestation or in rape. You can always illustrate by single incidences; you can always get an incidence. The newspapers will always help. You may find one rapist, and they found pornography in his room. And that means that pornography caused it. They also found milk in his refrigerator!

Porn Reduces Violence

Does porn cause violence? Clearly, no. In laboratory settings, viewing nonviolent sexually explicit material actually *reduces* aggressive tendencies. This suggests that nonviolent pornography can help reduce the rate of rape. In fact, that is exactly what happened when Denmark legalized pornography: Rape rates went down, and then stabilized at a lower level.

Al Goldstein, *Los Angeles Times*, February 8, 1989.

I am not playing games because I am angry. We are all against pornography. It is evil. But it is a *symptom* of the kind of society in which we live. It doesn't cause anything. The sooner we get away from the rhetoric, the sooner we will begin to understand that, if we put 10 percent of the energy that we put against pornography into positive programs such as sex education in the schools, we can have an effect. All we need is three people in any program in the United States and there is no sex education. All you need is one Eagle Forum woman or man in one school system, and the program is finished. We have enough energy among our fellow humanists to create a whole new curriculum. All they have is one or two or three people—we have usually eleven. We don't need twelve, because you are going to lose one anyway. We haven't understood the power that we have. Are we going to use this power in unity with the worst, most corrupt elements in our society, such as the Eagle Forum and the Moral Majority? Are we going to join them and give them more power? Because they are going to use that. I warn you: they are going to use this power against us, and the feminists are going to be the first victims. Thank you.

"The case for prohibition . . . seems to be quite strong regardless of whether pornography can be shown to be among the many causes of crime."

Pornography Should Be Prohibited

Ernest van den Haag

The First Amendment guarantees Americans freedom of speech, and of the press, and it is interpreted by some to cover all forms of expression, including pornography. In the following viewpoint, Ernest van den Haag argues that pornography is not worthy of this protection. He claims that pornography erodes the social bonds that connect us to other members of society, thereby causing crime. Van den Haag is John M. Olin Professor of Jurisprudence and Public Policy at Fordham University in New York.

As you read, consider the following questions:

1. According to van den Haag, what is wrong with the feminist interpretation of pornography?
2. How does the author think pornography affects those who read it?
3. How does van den Haag respond to the fears that censorship will lead to a police state?

Ernest van den Haag,"Pornography and the Law," *The Heritage Lectures #111,* published by The Heritage Foundation in 1987.

The Meese Commission report on pornography was released in 1986 and is now old hat. Perhaps this is a good time to examine with some detachment the question on which it sought to shed light: Should we continue to outlaw pornography while, in effect, tolerating it? Should we legalize it? Or should we find a method of outlawing it effectively?

For those who wish to legalize pornography the answer is simple. Whether or not pornography is distasteful or morally harmful, it affects only those who buy it. The government is not in charge of their morals. It is part of one's freedom to make choices that are harmful to oneself or disapproved by others. Those offended by pornography can readily refrain. There is no need for the law to protect them; no one compels them to see X-rated movies or buy pornographic magazines. Legitimate questions about advertising, public visibility, and access by children are marginal and could be solved by such measures as plain wrappers and inconspicuous signs.

Surely the people who want to legalize pornography are right if, as they contend, pornography does no harm to those who do not volunteer to buy it. This is the question the Meese Commission addressed. The Commission has been ridiculed by all the usual "civil libertarians." However, if one actually looks at its report, one finds that the Commission did quite reasonable work in trying to answer the question it focused on: Does pornography lead to crime? If it does, obviously it harms persons who did not volunteer for the harm. They are entitled to protection, provided that protection is consistent with constitutional principles.

The Commission decided that pornography, particularly sado-masochistic pornography, stimulates, to say the least, sex crimes. One can argue about this. There is a chicken and egg problem. Does the prospective rapist consume pornography because he independently is a prospective rapist, or is it the pornography which causes, or stimulates, a disposition to rape that did not pre-exist or was minor? Which comes first? However, there seems to be little doubt that a disposition to commit sex crimes may be strengthened or activated by pornography, which appears to legitimize them and to weaken internal restraints.

Changing Sexual Mores

The general evidence strongly suggests that crime can be stimulated by communications, ideas and sensations aroused by movies or books. Few sayings are as silly as the *dictum* attributed to Jimmy Walker (the late New York mayor) to the effect that "No girl has ever been seduced by a book." Books do not seduce directly any more than whiskey does. But they help. After all, even if one discounts the "sexual revolution," one cannot deny that sexual mores have changed over time, owing not to changes in biology, but to changed ideas and sentiments that infect people and lead them to action. Books such as the Bible or *Das Kapital* influence people's actions because of the ideas they expound. Pornography, which is bereft of ideas, influences people because of the sensations and attitudes it stimulates. It is consumed for the sake of these sensations as drugs are and may influence actions analogously.

But pornography is not the only thing that may lead to sex crime, and certainly it does so only sometimes. Many people consume it without being led to crime. Others become criminals without pornography. Further, alcohol too may lead to crime, or TV violence—indeed myriad things. We cannot outlaw everything, not even every communication, that sometimes leads to crime. Why then outlaw pornography?

Regulating Lust

There is manifestly an appetite for porn. There are people willing to cater to this appetite. Why should not the willing buyer and the willing seller enter into conventional arrangements?

Surely the reason is that lust is an appetite that needs to be regulated. We live in a free society that, just to begin with, regulates that appetite by authorizing only a single marriage at one time.

William F. Buckley Jr., *National Review*, August 29, 1986.

If the Meese Commission conclusion—let's prohibit pornography because it may lead to crime—does not quite follow from its evidence, the idea of some feminists that pornography is a male conspiracy against females to exploit them, and foster, or help, violence against them, is even less well founded. Pornography exploits sex, not females. The criminal effects are not intended, let alone conspired for. Women are accidental. Pornographers would be just as willing to present pictures of males as of females if there were a market for them. There isn't, except for male homosexuals, who indeed are catered to by pornographers. Most females—be it for cultural, psychological, or biological reasons—do not seem to want to consume pornography. Actually males, who spend good money for the stuff, are more, not less, exploited than the females who earn it. At any rate, I can't see exploitation (a cloudy concept to begin with, meaning not much more than "I don't like it"), since both buyers and sellers volunteer and both have alternatives. They do what they want to do; they are not compelled to do it. Exploitation without compulsion is hard to figure out.

O.K., forget about the feminists. Why should we punish the sale of pornography? (Nobody advocates prior restraint, censorship, which is a pseudo-issue.) The Meese Commission reason, that it may lead to crime, is not sufficient. Are there other reasons? I believe there are. The social damage pornography does is greater, yet more diffuse than indicated by individual crimes. Just as chemical pollution may erode stones, statues, and buildings, so pornography erodes civility and our social institutions.

Avoiding Art and Humanity

By definition, pornography deindividualizes and dehumanizes sexual acts. By eliminating the contexts it reduces males and females simply to bearers of impersonal sensations of pleasure and pain. This dehumanization eliminates the empathy that restrains us ultimately from sadism and non-consensual acts. The cliche-language and the stereotyped situations of characters not characterized, except sexually, are defining characteristics of pornography. The pornographer avoids distraction from the masturbatory fantasy by avoiding art and humanity. Art may "cancel lust" (as Santayana thought) or sublimate it. The pornographer desublimates it. Those who resort to pornographic fantasies habitually are people who are ungratified by others (for endogenous or external reasons). They seek gratification in using others, in inflicting pain (sometimes in suffering it), at least in their fantasy. In this respect, *The Story of O,* which, itself pornographic, also depicts the rather self-defeating outcome of pornographic fantasy, is paradigmatic.

In a sense, pornographic and finally sadistic literature is antihuman. Were it directed against a specific human group—e.g., Jews or Blacks—the same liberal ideologues who now oppose outlawing pornography might advocate prohibiting it. Should we find a little black or Jewish girl tortured to death and her death agony taped by her murderers, and should we find the murderers imbued with sadistic anti-Semitic or anti-black literature, most liberals would advocate that the circulation of such literature be prohibited. Why should humanity as such be less protected than any of the specific groups that compose it? That the sexualized hate articulated is directed against people in general, rather than against only Jews or Negroes, makes it no less dangerous; on the contrary; it makes it as dangerous to more people.

But shouldn't an adult be able to control himself and read or see, without enacting, what he knows to be wrong or, at least, illegal? Perhaps he should. But we are not dealing with a homogeneous group called grown-ups nor is it possible in the modern American environment to limit anything to adults. Children and adolescents are not supervised enough. Further, the authority of their supervisors has been diminished too much to make effective supervision possible. As for grown-ups, many are far from the self-restrained healthy type envisaged by democratic theory. They may easily be given a last, or first, push by the materials I would like to see prohibited.

Now, if these materials had artistic, indeed any but pornographic value, we would have to weigh the loss against the importance of avoiding their deleterious influence. We may even be ready to sacrifice some probable victims for the sake of this value. But pornographic "literature" is without literary value. It is printed, but it is not literature. Else it cannot be defined as pornography. Hence there is nothing to be lost by restricting it, and much to be gained.

Affects the Quality of Life

Self-restrained and controlled individuals exist and function in an environment which fosters reasonable conduct. But few such individuals will be created, and they will function less well, in an environment where they receive little social support, where sadistic acts are openly held up as models and sadistic fantasies are sold to any purchaser. To be sure, a virtuous man will not commit adultery. But a wise wife will avoid situations where the possibility is alluring and the opportunity available. Why must society lead its members into temptation and then punish them when they do what they were tempted to do? But more than individual cases are at issue.

Pornography affects the quality of our lives. It depreciates emotional ties and individual relationships in favor of fungible ones, in which physical pleasure is, in principle, separated from any emotional or even personal relationships. Yet, without "emotional ties which hold the group together," according to Freud there is "the cessation of all feelings of consideration" and therewith social disintegration and crime. "Emotional ties" are systematically depreciated by pornography.

Limits to Free Speech

Long ago legal experts recognized that free speech should not include the right to slander and defame. Among the practitioners of slander and defamation are racists and pornographers.

Free speech does not include freedom to malign or demean. Although there are some fine lines here that need further definition, the banning of violence-related pornography is not censorship.

People's Daily World, July 16, 1986.

Thus pornography undermines the social bond on which human association—from family to nation—must depend. It is this social bond which deters most of us, most of the time, from using our neighbors as we please, without regard to their own preferences. We are taught, and most of us learn, to perceive others as ends in themselves and not merely as means to our pleasure. This learning is the basis of society. Yet it is precarious. We need to be socialized continuously. Pornography undermines the internal restraints on which society must depend and which the criminal law with its sanctions can reinforce but not create. This seems quite enough to limit pornography (we will never succeed in doing more). No need (or possibility) to prove a direct and unavoidable relationship to crime. Such a direct causal relationship is likely occasionally, perhaps often. But it is largely beside the point when compared to the erosion of the social bond.

I prefer to live in a society in which public invitations to do without love in individual relationships, to regress to an infantile level of sexuality, stripped of emotion, are not consistently extended. Such invitations are all too likely to be tempting. We all are vulnerable to regression. After all, each of us developed laboriously and with much social effort from anti-social infants into acceptable adults. Invitations to regression should not be socially endorsed. Wherefore the case for prohibition of obscenity seems to be quite strong regardless of whether pornography can be shown to be among the many causes of crime.

Pornography Not Protected

Interstate commerce in pornography is already illegal under federal statutes, and intrastate pornography is illegal in most states. As interpreted by the Supreme Court the First Amendment does not protect pornography, defined as that which:

1) taken as whole predominantly appeals to the prurient interest (a morbid interest in sex); and

2) lacks serious literary, scientific, artistic, or political value (i.e. does not predominantly offer new ideas or aesthetic experiences); and

3) describes sexual conduct in ways judged to be patently offensive by the standards of the community in which the material is sold.

These legal criteria are rather porous. For instance, the depiction of intercourse with animals may be legal, since it may not appeal to the prurient interest of the average person. The depiction of excretion may be legal, since it may not appeal to the prurient interest of the average person either. The standards of the local community are vague (and costly to ascertain), unless the jury is taken to mean the community. The court could have been more concrete and specific.

Further, present law requires that the material at issue be considered "as a whole" to determine whether it "predominantly" appeals to the prurient interest. This makes perfect sense for, say, novels, works meant to be taken as a whole, but no sense for periodicals, which, by definition, consist of independent articles or pictures. Why should it not be sufficient if some pictures, or other contributions, to a periodical are obscene, even if the rest consists of non-obscene essays? The non-obscene material usually serves as camouflage or pretense. For a movie, if more than 5 percent of its running time is devoted to images which, taken in isolation, would be regarded as obscene, the movie should be so regarded.

No First Amendment Protection

Traditionally pornography has not been thought to be protected by the First Amendment. The idea that the First Amendment licenses pornographers, though widespread, is quite recent. It has no legal basis. Further, the First Amendment prohibits only abridging freedom of speech and of the press. Yet current interpretations have led the courts to conclude that the First Amendment protects "expression" (such as nude dancing) as well. Although expression, dancing is certainly not speech, let alone print. Nothing in the First Amendment protects speechless expression, such as music or dance, or for that matter, pictures.

Breaking Porn's Back

One of the major factors in the growth of the pornography traffic is the lack of vigorous enforcement of obscenity laws, particularly at the federal level. . . .

Continuous, vigorous enforcement of the law is the answer. When arrests and prosecutions begin, the sex industry is put on warning. Prison sentences, fines, legal fees will put the pornographers out of business. Atlanta, Jacksonville and Cincinnati are clean cities because of vigorous, continuous enforcement of the law. And experts say that with aggressive enforcement of federal law, the back of the porno industry would be broken in 18 months.

"Cliché Arguments," *Morality in Media, Inc.*

Thus, in accordance with the First Amendment, legislatures cannot abridge the communication of information or of ideas. But pornography as defined by the courts is bereft of either. Legislatures can constitutionally allow pornography or nude dancing, but they need not. The legal question is not, can we prohibit pornography? (The answer is yes.) What is in dispute in each case is only: Is this material obscene according to the legal definition given above?

Of course there will be doubtful cases—but no more so than in other areas of the law. Courts exist to decide doubtful cases and can do so in this area as well as in any other. Standards of obscenity vary over time. Yet at any time there are standards discoverable by the courts. There is no great difficulty in discerning them—as lawyers are aware, though they often pretend otherwise. Yet, although often professing to be unable to distinguish obscene from non-obscene material, lawyers do not expose their genitals in court. They must have some knowledge of prevailing standards.

Depiction of the nude body, even in alluring poses, is no longer regarded as offensive. Nor is explicit prose. Visual depictions that focus on the genitals—rather than to merely include them—are. Detailed and explicit visual depictions of genital actions, including copulation, masturbation, and depiction of genital arousal, are prurient and offensive. So are prurient depictions which make public what traditionally has been private and intimate.

Making Distinctions

The perception of pornographic qualities in any work depends on literary or aesthetic criticism. Therefore, some argue, it is a matter of opinion. In court, serious critics often behave as though they believed criticism to be a matter of opinion. But why be a critic—and teach in universities—if it involves no more than uttering capricious and arbitrary opinions? If criticism cannot tell pornography from literature, what can it tell us? Of course, critics may disagree; so do other witnesses, including psychiatrists and handwriting experts. The decision is up to the courts; the literary witnesses only have the obligation to testify truthfully as to what is, or is not, pornography.

Some of the critics who claim that they cannot make the distinction do not wish to, because they regard pornography as legitimate; others fear that censorship of pornography may be extended to actual literature. Whatever the merits of such views (I don't see any), they do not justify testifying that the distinction cannot be made. A witness is not entitled to deny that he saw what he did see, simply to save the accused from a punishment he dislikes. A critic who is really incapable of distinguishing pornography from literature certainly has no business being one; a critic who is capable of making the distinction has no business testifying that he is not.

Oh, yes, there is one bugaboo: A "police state," it is feared, may develop from prohibiting the sale of pornography and punishing violators. That argument is not too plausible. . . . No democracy has ever become a police state by using the criminal law to restrain obscenity. The Weimar Republic in Germany was not replaced by Nazism because it did. It did not. Once Hitler was in power, he used it to abolish all freedom and to institute censorship.

"Religious beliefs and determinations of morality cannot dictate what is permissible for man to read, think, fantasize—be it the classics or 'smut.'"

Pornography Should Not Be Prohibited

Spartacist League and Partisan Defense Committee

The Spartacist League calls itself a revolutionary organization committed to the victory of the socialist revolution in the US. In the following viewpoint the League joins forces with the Partisan Defense Committee, another socialist organization, to argue against anti-pornography laws. They believe that prohibiting pornography is censorship and contend that people have a right to view pornography.

As you read, consider the following questions:

1. Why do the authors object to family values?
2. Why do the authors believe obscenity is not an exception to the First Amendment?
3. What is wrong with the Supreme Court's definition of obscenity, according to the authors?

Spartacist League and Partisan Defense Committee, "No to RICO Sex Witchhunt," *Women and Revolution*. Summer 1988. Reprinted with permission.

On May 12, 1988 the Spartacist League and Partisan Defense Committee filed an *amici curiae* (friends of the court) legal brief in the Supreme Court opposing state use of draconian RICO (Racketeer Influenced and Corrupt Organizations) conspiracy laws to shut down publishers and distributors of allegedly "obscene" material. The SL and PDC are supporting the appeal of Indiana booksellers against a state RICO law under which their bookstores were padlocked and all their assets seized simply on a judge's determination that there was "probable cause" to believe the stores had sold two or more "obscene products." . . .

We reprint below excerpts from the SL/PDC brief.

The issue presented in these cases is whether the government can criminalize First Amendment communicative materials, seize and destroy them and imprison their distributors—simply by alleging "obscenity." In these cases the government applied the most powerful weapon in its legal arsenal to an area of social concern inseparably connected to humanity's most public and most private worlds—opinion and sex. The current battleground is personal freedoms—focused on the three-letter word "sex." The battle cry of the government and its religious surrogates is the "protection of morality, family, children."

Government's Frontal Assault

These cases represent government's frontal assault on First Amendment protection of the spoken and written word, books, films, and the right to publish and distribute communicative material. The starting point is the current majority position of the Supreme Court that the First Amendment is not an absolute—that an "obscenity" exception exists. The established tests for "obscenity" are subjective, imbued with religious considerations, and justified on the basis of a false history of the First Amendment obscenity exception.

Thus these cases pose in stark relief whether the First Amendment is fact or fiction; whether by an Orwellian turn of phrase books, magazines, and video movies can be transformed from First Amendment materials to fruits of racketeering.

The Spartacist League seeks to act, as Lenin described the role of the vanguard workers party, as a "tribune of the people." Thus the Spartacist League opposes *all* aspects of social oppression, whether stemming from race and national hatred or from the repressive sexual morality enforced by the state and bourgeois family.

Social bigotry, racism and religion are the ideological concomitants of the drive against "godless communism" abroad and blacks, minorities and unions at home. There is a desire by the American rulers to recreate the reactionary environment of the 1950s—the first and last decade of the American century—a period pre-Vietnam, pre-"sexual liberation," pre-civil rights movement and above all pre-American capitalism's loss of world economic and military hegemony.

Anti-Porn, Anti-Women

As Marxists, *amici curiae* are defenders of democratic rights, recognizing the root cause of the contraction of constitutionally protected rights lies in the class nature of the state. Harold Laski explains in his treatise *The State in Theory and Practice* (1935):

> How accidental was the union of capitalism with democracy. It was the outcome, not of an essential harmony of inner principle, but of that epoch in economic evolution when capitalism was in its phase of expansion. It had conferred political power upon the masses; but it was upon the saving condition that political power should not be utilized to cut at the root of capitalist postulates. It would offer social reforms so long as these did not jeopardize the essential relations of the capitalist system. When they did as occurred in the post-war [World War I] years, the contradiction between capitalism and democracy became the essential institutional feature of Western civilization.

As materialists, *amici curiae* understand that attempts today to proscribe sexuality and particular sexual practices (and their depiction in pornography) necessarily reflect the attitudes, values and prejudices shaped by this class society. Most prominent is the hypocritical glorification of the monogamous family unit, which Marxists have classically defined as the main Western social institution oppressing women. The "family values" the pornography police claim to uphold are in fact justification for depriving women of equal status not only in the marketplace but in relation to their own bodies.

Bad Politics

Banning porn is bad politics. It threatens something radicals ought to be proprietary about: free speech. It threatens privacy and it threatens free choice about sexuality.

Guardian, October 23, 1985.

Pre-eminent American novelist and social commentator Gore Vidal has aptly stated "sex is politics" noting that:

> Sexual attitudes of any given society are the result of political decisions. . . .Today Americans are in a state of terminal hysteria on the subject of sex in general and of homosexuality in particular because the owners of the country regard the family as the last means of control over those who work and consume.
> —"Sex Is Politics," *The Second American Revolution* (1982)

Those whose private sexual life does not conform to the official values of "Judeo-Christianity" and this capitalist state are subject to heavy penalties, as the decision of [the Supreme Court] upholding sodomy laws in Georgia—which specifically made reference to biblical tradition—made clear. Censoring sexual expression via video, print or photograph is a continuation of this sex witchhunt.

Crimes Without Victims

The Spartacist League has a longstanding position against government regulation of private life. As stated in the Spartacist League document *Youth, Class and Party* (1971), " . . . we call for an end to all laws against what are known as 'crimes without victims' (e.g., prostitution, pornography, gambling, drug addiction, anti-liquor laws). . . . Laws against gambling and various sexual practices reflect official puritanism allied to organized religion, which acts as an important ideological pillar of capitalism, convincing the masses there can be no happiness this side of the grave."

Certainly some pornography reflects the frustrations and hostilities engendered by this repressive society. *Amici curiae* do not advocate any particular sexual practices, but define their position essentially in the negative: against this state's attempts to censor, limit and cripple human sexual expression in the service of its own reactionary ideology.

People have the right to read or look at whatever they want, to write, paint or film it too, and to engage in whatever sexual practices (or none at all) they choose, so long as they're consensual. The point is neither to proscribe, nor prescribe, what kind of sex people "should" have.

No Obscenity Precedent

Constitutional history discloses that particularly when the populace is being prepared for war, the protections of the First Amendment are ignored. And, in the midst of a national hysteria around AIDS, in *Bowers v. Hardwick* . . . [the Supreme Court] upheld Georgia's sodomy law, criminalizing particular sex acts between consenting adults, homosexuals and heterosexuals alike, in the privacy of home.

However, judicial claims that "implicit in the history of the First Amendment is the rejection of obscenity as utterly without redeeming social importance," are simply and clearly erroneous. There is no judicial precedent from British common law or the new American republic regarding prosecution of obscenity. . . . Reported common law prosecutions were based not on concerns of sexual improprieties but political and religious themes, particularly an attack on the state religion. . . . Thus, in the words of Mr. Justice Douglas "the creation of the 'obscenity' exception to the First Amendment was a legislative and judicial *tour de force*."

160

Criminalization of purportedly obscene writings has significantly peaked at key periods of social change. . . . It was not until the period of post-Reconstruction reaction that Congress passed legislation relating to obscenity. After the Civil War, mass printing, literacy, second-class postal rates, combined with the presence of single men living outside family supervision in the cities provided a market for sexual commerce. "An Act for the Suppression of Trade in, and Circulation of Obscene Literature and Articles of Immoral Use," had as its object the specific prohibition of advertising and mailing of birth control information. This Act . . . was promulgated by one Anthony Comstock who personally supervised its enforcement as an unpaid postal inspector. . . . It took the concerted campaign of Margaret Sanger to make birth control information available to women to defeat Comstock and his cronies in the Societies for the Suppression of Vice, Women's Christian Temperance Union, and the YMCA, forty years later.

Supporting Freedom

Like it or not, we must support the rights of the pornographers to sell their wares. Or who knows who will be next? It is the same position in which one finds oneself when it is necessary to give a parade permit to the Ku Klux Klan. Thomas Paine summed it all up when he said "Those who expect to reap the blessings of freedom must undergo the fatigue of supporting it."

Jon G. Murray, *American Atheist*, June 1986.

Post World War II, Cold War politics found expression in sexual politics—preoccupation with family stability, "internal subversion," "moral fiber" and "decency." The focus of the Courts turned to commercial distribution of allegedly obscene materials—books, magazines, and more recently video movies.

This Court has not found it possible to arrive at an objective legal standard of obscenity. The court-established standards are imbued with religious, moral and subjective literary determinations. . . .

Religious beliefs and determinations of morality cannot dictate what is permissible for man to read, think, fantasize—be it the classics or "smut" erotica or pornography. Absent physical harm to another, it is no concern of the state. Established First Amendment law does not permit religious or moral determination of "public consensus."

Recognizing Statements That Are Provable

From various sources of information we are constantly confronted with statements and generalizations about social and moral problems. In order to think clearly about these problems, it is useful if one can make a basic distinction between statements for which evidence can be found and other statements which cannot be verified or proved because evidence is not available, or the issue is so controversial that it cannot be definitely proved.

Readers should be aware that magazines, newspapers, and other sources often contain statements of a controversial nature. The following activity is designed to allow experimentation with statements that are provable and those that are not.

The following statements are taken from the viewpoints in this chapter. Consider each statement carefully. *Mark P for any statement you believe is provable. Mark U for any statement you feel is unprovable because of the lack of evidence. Mark C for any statements you think are too controversial to be proved to everyone's satisfaction.*

If you are doing this activity as a member of a class or group, compare your answers with those of other class or group members. Be able to defend your answers. You may discover that others will come to different conclusions than you do. Listening to the reasons others present for their answers may give you valuable insights in recognizing statements that are provable.

P = *provable*
U = *unprovable*
C = *too controversial*

162

1. Banning pornography will end violence against women.

2. Often women are coerced or forced into performing for pornography.

3. Banning pornography will eventually lead to a police state.

4. Pornography that portrays sexual violence causes sexual violence.

5. The Meese Commission report on pornography was released in 1986.

6. Americans have the right to do whatever they want in the privacy of their own homes.

7. *Penthouse* in December of 1984 was distributing photographs of women being tightly bound, hanging from trees and pegs.

8. Bob Guccione produced a magazine called *Viva* in 1972.

9. Pornography has no literary value.

10. The Eagle Forum and the Moral Majority are the most corrupt elements of our society.

11. Margaret Sanger campaigned in the early years of the century for women's right to birth control.

12. Some radical feminists believe that men are by nature violent.

13. On May 12, 1988 the Spartacist League filed a legal brief in the Supreme Court opposing the use of draconian laws to shut down publishers.

14. The artists of ancient Greece, India, and Japan produced a lot of sexually explicit art.

15. If we all learned self-restraint, pornography would not be a problem.

16. A desire for pornography is a natural part of a man's sexuality.

17. Obscenity laws do not protect women because they are created by a sexist society and so must be sexist.

18. Edward Donnerstein said that there can be demonstrated a causal relationship between exposure to porn and effects on attitudes.

Periodical Bibliography

The following articles have been selected to supplement the diverse views presented in this chapter.

Vern L. Bullough   "On Ted Bundy, Pornography, and Capital Punishment," *Free Inquiry*, Spring 1989. Available from the Council for Democratic and Secular Humanism, 3159 Bailey Ave., Buffalo, NY 14215.

Robert Corn-Revere   "Putting the First out of Business," *The Nation*, September 26, 1988.

Jean Davidson   "What's So Obscene About Pornography?" *U.S. Catholic*, June 1988.

Barbara Deane   "Wrong Number!" *Family Circle*, February 1, 1989.

Barbara Grizzuti Harrison   "Dirty Dialing: Sex Is Only a Phone Call Away," *Mademoiselle*, July 1988.

Bill Hybels   "The Sin That So Easily Entangles," *Moody Monthly*, April 1989.

Bruce E. Johansen   "The Meese Police on Porn Patrol," *The Progressive*, June 1988.

Michael S. Kimmel   "Pornography and Its Discontents," *Psychology Today*, February 1988.

Maria Laurino   "A Strange Pair of Experts," *Ms.*, December 1988.

Robert W. Lee   "Waging War on Smut," *Conservative Digest*, November 1988.

Art Levine and Kathleen Currie   "Whip Me, Beat Me, and While You're at It Cancel My NOW Membership," *The Washington Monthly*, June 1987.

Connaught Marshner   "How Don Wildmon Is Beating the Princes of Porn," *Conservative Digest*, March 1988.

Phyllis Schlafly   "Pornography's Victims," *The Phyllis Schlafly Report*, April 1987. Available from the Eagle Trust Fund, Box 618, Alton, IL 62002.

Lawrence A. Stanley   "The Child-Pornography Myth," *Playboy*, September 1988.

Terry Teachout   "The Pornography Report That Never Was," *Commentary*, August 1987.

What Sexual Philosophy Is Best?

Chapter Preface

Today a wide variety of sexual relationships are common, from committed to noncommitted relationships, heterosexuality, homosexuality, and bisexuality. The debate about what type of sexual relationship is best remains heated.

Those who advocate nontraditional relationships believe they allow people freedom and fulfillment. They see the variety of alternatives available to people today as a beneficial and radical break from the past.

Supporters of more traditional relationships hold that monogamy demonstrates respect and honesty and is thus healthier than alternative relationships. According to this view, new sexual mores are harmful.

The sexual philosophies discussed in the following chapter represent the continuing debate between those who favor traditional views on sexuality and their opponents.

"Virginity is a safe, viable, fulfilling alternative."

Virginity Is Fulfilling

Neal Bernards

A common view is that the sexual revolution made virginity not only outdated but ridiculous in the eyes of popular culture. Neal Bernards, the author of the following viewpoint, describes his experiences working as a supervisory aide at Hopkins High School in Hopkins, Minnesota. He writes that many of the teenagers at the high school had sex before they were ready for it because they felt social pressure to lose their virginity. Bernards believes that his own decision to remain a virgin and save himself for marriage is a healthy choice in the age of AIDS and herpes. Bernards is a free-lance writer and editor in St. Paul, Minnesota.

As you read, consider the following questions:

1. Why does the author believe that not having sexual intercourse until his wedding night will improve his marriage?
2. How does Bernards' girlfriend view his choice to remain a virgin?
3. What are the benefits of remaining a virgin, according to the author?

Neal Bernards, "A Sojourn Through the Sexual Landscape of America," a position paper, July 12, 1989.

Sex is natural—sex is good
Not everybody does it
But everybody should.
George Michael, "I Want Your Sex," 1987.

George Michael is right, not everyone does it. However, I disagree that everyone should. Fifteen-year-old girls should not have sex. Immature boys with no employable skills should not have sex. I should not have sex, at least not now.

I am a 26-year-old male virgin who is saving himself for marriage. That makes me a rarity in these days when our popular culture tells us that sex is the end-all and be-all of existence. Like the chemical soma in Aldous Huxley's *Brave New World*, sex has become America's drug of choice. Sex is entertainment, a replacement for love, and an advertising tool. Those who wish not to partake are viewed as aberrant, abnormal, and even dangerous. It's as though we abstainers are not buying into the American dream.

And not participating in guilt-free, easy-access sex is hard for most people to understand, especially adolescents. My work as an administrative aide in a suburban high school has led to many conversations with teenagers about sex. High school students are often skeptical when I tell them I'm still a virgin at age 26. They've become so overwhelmed by the sexual messages of society that they cannot conceive of a man who isn't sexually active. Generally, it takes at least ten minutes of convincing before the teenager I've spoken with will believe that I'm not simply holding the "just say no" line because I'm supposed to be a responsible role model. One particularly experienced senior commented, "But sex is so much fun. You don't know what you're missing." To which I replied, "Yes, I do know what I'm missing, but I think it's worth it."

It's worth it to me because I know that when I do finally have intercourse, it will be for the right reasons. I'll do it for love, for pleasure, and as a sign of commitment. In this era of a 50 percent divorce rate, the exclusive bond of sexual intercourse created between my wife and me may help strengthen our marriage. By experiencing sex for the first time on my wedding night, I hope to communicate to my wife that I have saved something special for her. That she is different from all my other relationships. My virginity won't guarantee a smooth ride to my twenty-fifth wedding anniversary, but it won't hurt.

Teens' Ruined Lives

What hurts is the sight of a semi-literate 17-year-old and her newborn baby boy who are forced to live without proper food or enough money. Or the honor student who cannot attend college because she must work to support her child. One of the more disturbing moments at the high school came when I searched an attractive, blonde 16-year-old girl for drugs. Instead of finding illegal drugs or paraphernalia, I found cigarettes and her birth-control pills. (I must add that I firmly support the use of contraception by sexually active teens.) What disturbed me is that I knew the type of abusive, irresponsible boys she hung out with and these boys' attitudes toward the girls they "dated." She felt pressure to have sex with these boys to be accepted. That kind of thinking is tragically prevalent among American teens today.

Caring and Commitment

Remember those childhood dreams of a deep and growing romance, candle-lit dinners, soft conversations? The joyous wedding in which the groom watched, stars in his eyes, as his lovely bride walked down the aisle to join him? Or the "happily ever after" that always followed?

Can a case be made for sex with deep caring and commitment, to be enjoyed and to strengthen a permanent marriage relationship? We say yes!

Yes, we do need to be mature and realistic in our expectations about love and marriage. But much of what we all long for is available in a relationship that grows from warm friendship to love to marriage and then to sex.

Built on the right foundation, physical intimacy means so much more. Sex strengthens the bond between married couples because it's exclusive. The emotional and sexual love shared on the wedding night ought to be just the beginning of a meaningful life together filled with deepening love and sexual enjoyment.

Michael Bennett and Rebecca Bennett, *The Plain Truth*, April 1989.

But what does that have to do with me, a man well beyond his teens? It means that I can set an example and tell teenagers it's possible to resist the influences that advocate premarital sex and that they can make a rational decision to abstain.

Admittedly, my thinking about sex is the result of an evangelical Christian upbringing that condemned premartial sex as sinful. But my sexual philosophy is based on more that that. The rigid moral upbringing of my youth evolved into a personal conviction that took me through the teen years into early adulthood. Initially I refrained from intercourse out of a fear of divine punishment, but then I came to see sex as a personal choice. I realized that God would not strike me dead if I had sex, nor would my peers force me into sex against my will. As I got older I started to take pride in the fact that I could escape both the religious guilt surrounding sex and the societal pressures to be sexually active.

To be honest, my convictions were rarely tested in high school because I dated girls with similar sexual philosophies. The opportunity for intercourse either rarely came up or was such a taboo subject that its possibility was never even broached. In college my dating horizons started to expand, but the women in the Baptist school I attended were generally more interested in finding husbands than having good sex. So while I did my share of making out in the backseat, it rarely progressed to the point where sex was discussed. If it was discussed, I either begged off or explained that I was a virgin and intended to stay that way.

Sexual Assumptions

The post-collegiate dating years have been the toughest. Where in my youth I rarely had to explain myself, now I must. Women assume that all men my age are sexually active and are very surprised when they learn I'm not. They find it difficult to believe that any modern male, aside from priests and religious fundamentalists, is still a virgin this late in life. However, most people respect my decision to remain a virgin until marriage and keep the ridicule to a minimum. The women I've dated who were no longer virgins showed little interest in deflowering me. Conversely, they actually said that they'd feel bad if they took my virginity from me.

The downside of abstinence is that I've consciously avoided becoming close to some women because I knew the issue of sex would arise and I couldn't face their questions. I didn't want to justify my beliefs to someone I know wouldn't be sympathetic. My abstinence has served as a sort of screening process to keep me from developing relationships with women who don't share my values, or at least understand them. No woman has ever stopped dating me because I wouldn't have intercourse, but that's because I generally terminated the relationship before they did.

My present relationship is working out well despite the fact that I'm a virgin and she is not. I realized that we could work out our differences when she said to a mutual friend, "Our relationship has been strengthened because we don't have sex. It's made me reconsider some of my past relationships and my views on sex before marriage. I now realize that Neal is interested in me as a person and not as a physical, sexual object." Though she would enjoy the intimacy of intercourse and does not fully understand my decision, she accepts my choice and does not press the issue.

Even with the daily temptations to have sex, the fact that I've reached age 26 with my virginity intact would make it extremely difficult for me to violate the moral standards I've set for myself. Though I no longer believe the religious restrictions against sex are important, my virginity has become such an integral part of my identity that I cannot let it go. It's as if my personal moral structure would collapse if I changed my mind. All these years of saying no would lose their meaning if in one moment I decided to say yes. Moral convictions are such a rarity these days that I view my abstinence as a test of will. It's satisfying to know that, whatever else happens to me, I have the power to control one aspect of my life. No amount of breathless panting or sweaty pawing in the heat of passion will change my mind because too much thought and too much energy has gone into this decision.

A Guaranteed Commitment

Although a committed relationship may entail authentic love, the expression of that love in sexual consummation cannot be in the best interests of those involved unless the commitment is guaranteed to be authentic and protective of the parties (and of future progeny) through the marriage covenant. Sexual celebration of such a commitment is therefore reserved for marriage.

Premature and promiscuous sexual exchanges expose one to a variety of serious risks and dangers:
1. The risk of out-of-wedlock pregnancies and a variety of sexually transmitted diseases.
2. These consume the time and energy needed for personal development at a crucial juncture in the process of maturing, that is, at the time of adolescence. They generally entail an unhealthy emotional dependence on one person, at a time when a variety of friendships with many other persons of the same age should be cultivated.

Bishops of the Diocese of Erie, Pennsylvania, *Origins*, June 23, 1988.

No discussion of sexual abstinence would be complete without mention of AIDS and herpes. I am absolutely certain that I'm free from any taint of sexual disease. Few people can claim that. I don't mean to be smug, but it's offensive when public service ads announce that anyone can contract AIDS. Anyone cannot. I cannot, unless they mean to fan the hysteria and misinformation surrounding AIDS by saying it spreads through dirty toilet seats and mosquito bites. Absolute abstinence means absolute protection.

Abstinence also means protection from any chance of impregnation. Until I'm willing to provide lifetime support to a child, I will not have sex. To me, intercourse implies a commitment that translates into a willingness to spend a lifetime with my partner and/or the children we create. So far I've been unwilling to make that commitment. In my ten years of dating, I've had over twenty relationships of varying lengths and quality. If I'd had sex with even half of those women, I might now be a father, prematurely married, very ill, or extremely guilt-ridden. Short-term relationships are tricky enough without the emotional and psychological baggage that goes with intercourse.

All this is not to say that I lead a sex-free existence or am sexually frustrated. If I have told high school students anything about sex, it is that many alternatives exist to intercourse. One need not risk pregnancy or sexually transmitted diseases to find intimacy and sexual satisfaction. Published research on sexual expression indicates that intercourse often is used to gain intimacy when hugging and holding your partner would work as well. For sexual activity the researchers advocate mutual masturbation, which is a pretty good alternative to intercourse and its unwanted effects: pregnancy and debilitating disease.

Going All the Way

I may be an endangered species, but I know that I am not alone in my abstinence, especially as the fear of AIDS continues to grow. Others share my conviction that virginity is a safe, viable, fulfilling alternative. My life is no more empty nor my relationships less meaningful because I abstain from sex. I simply choose to postpone intercourse until the safety and security of marriage. I've made it this far, why not go all the way?

"When a young man is in bed with a woman he desires, it is as if his entire life before that moment has been no more than preamble."

Sex Is Fulfilling

Frank Conroy

In the following viewpoint, Frank Conroy argues that sex is a rewarding experience. He also contends that sex can help men and women understand each other better because it leads to honest communication between partners. Conroy is a novelist who has written *Stop Time,* is addition to magazine articles for *Esquire, Harper's* and *The New York Times Magazine.*

As you read, consider the following questions:

1. According to Conroy, how do teenage boys relate to teenage girls?
2. What does Conroy describe as the benefits of passionate love?
3. According to the author, what are the limitations of passionate love?

Frank Conroy, "How Sex Feels: A Reverie," *Esquire*, June 1987. Reprinted by permission of the author.

Consider the boy. Any boy—the kid who packs bags at the supermarket after school, for instance. He has long been aware of the mysterious otherness of girls. But now he is drawn to a particular girl, the one with the brown hair who buys shampoo all the time. The boy is shy and risks considerable mortification in approaching her. He is astonished to find himself doing it. Surely she will ignore him, or worse yet, sense the fiend in him and turn away in disgust. It seems miraculous when she smiles.

So he is launched. Up to now it has been "girls," not a girl. To be sure, he has been in love many times—with movie stars, teachers, somebody's older sister—but always at a considerable distance. Buffeted between frank carnal hunger and the most rarefied romantic moonstruck agonies imaginable, he has till now really only loved an idea—the idea of the feminine, the other. Faced with a specific, individual girl, he must adjust.

The mating dance progresses. They meet, they hang out, go places together, laugh together, talk, explain themselves. Although his attention is total, more focused perhaps than ever before in his life, although he hangs on every word and can't take his eyes off her, his actual perception of her is dim. That is because he is looking at two things—the specific girl he has in front of him, whom he may or may not come to love, and the girlness embodied in her, which he has loved, and will love, all along.

The Impossible Event

And then one night, parked in some out of the way place, in the darkness . . . he begins to realize that the impossible event may well be about to occur. She has agreed to move to the back seat. Once there, things move along rapidly. Ever since he turned off the ignition the boy has been swept along by forces he can barely keep in check, the full power of which he has also sensed he must conceal from the girl, lest she be frightened away. He has pressed forward, but carefully, so as not to overwhelm her tacit right to control the tempo of events. Rather a gentle escalation, instinctively done, without guile, all the more remarkable considering that he is literally drunk with sensation and would have to think hard to remember whether it was Monday or Tuesday. He is in the midst of a storm, a great storm, and some kind of automatic pilot is guiding him. In the dark, chasing the girlness, he has almost forgotten the girl. He has been obsessed with getting her in the back seat, but by the time it happens his perception of her has narrowed to the point where he misses the fact that she actually wants to get in the back seat. He thinks it has all been the storm. His storm. His blindness is almost complete. . . .

Afterward, he is almost entirely absorbed by his own emotions. It seems a brand new world, after all. But stirring now, faintly,

174

as he watches the girl straighten her clothes, comb her hair, is the truly exotic idea that he might have something in common with her.

Consider the young man. By his mid-twenties, the dance has gotten more complicated. His male friends have gone off in a hundred different directions; there seem to be almost as many styles and attitudes toward women as there are individuals, and to make it more confusing, practically nobody talks about it. There are men who idealize women, men who fear them, men who use women, men who are used by them, men who pick women to impress their friends, men who pick their friends to impress their women, men who love them but don't like them, and on and on. The young man, as he watches all these guys he's known since high school, will notice an intensification of whatever character flaws were there to begin with, particularly in the presence of women. Even the most balanced individuals are taken over by various kinds of folly and self-delusion.

"Nanook believes that sex should be fun."

By now the young man realizes that women are different from one another. He no longer thinks that all you have to do is catch one to know everything. He has met women who don't seem to know any more about what it means to be a woman than he does. The matter is complex, to say the least. Each lover represents a facet of the greater feminine reality as he struggles to get some idea of the dimensions of that reality. By now he also knows there is no turning back. Alone, he is incomplete.

He takes the stairs three at a time, effortlessly, flying up to her apartment without a thought in his head. He feels light and alive.

If he felt any more alive he would lose contact with the earth altogether. The door opens and she is there, vividly there, more real than real.

He sits on the couch. She disappears into the kitchen while telling him a story about her cat. She keeps on talking while opening cupboards and delving into the refrigerator. Returning with drinks, she looks at him and her voice trails away. He hasn't moved, his eyes having held on the kitchen door until her reappearance. They simply look at each other, and in the silence there is an acknowledgment of what is going to happen.

He may feel a touch of that peculiar mixture of self-consciousness and expectation one feels in a concert hall moments before the music is to begin—a delicious, tense alertness, a sense of sliding inexorably through time toward that moment when the first chord will explode in the air. He says something inane, which breaks the spell, and she settles down beside him.

Too Good To Be True

Their talk rambles, almost as if they were noting things to talk about at some indeterminate time in the future. He is animated by curiosity—how does this fantastically complicated creature see the world? She likes Talking Heads? How wonderful and mysterious that she should like Talking Heads! Of course, a lot of people like them, but that doesn't matter, somehow. He imagines he can perceive her intent, her pure intent behind the words, as if the synapses of her brain were firing directly into his own.

As they touch each other, in any case, they gradually stop talking. Gestures that began as simple reflex become more complicated. Each moves toward a kind of immersion in the other, and they are like skiers gliding along a gentle slope, who feel themselves pulled faster as the slope increases. At a certain point they simply give over, they surrender and let themselves fly. . . .

When a young man is in bed with a woman he desires, it is as if his entire life before that moment has been no more than preamble. He feels himself to be at the exact center of the universe. He is not going somewhere, he is there. He is not waiting for something to happen, it is happening. It seems too good to be true, a fantastically lucky accident, a cosmic windfall. He's afraid that if he thinks about it, he'll lose it, so he doesn't think.

The Grand Passion

Consider the man, and in this case the lucky man, who has met, loved, and been loved by the right woman at the right time. He may marry this woman if he isn't married already, but probably not, because special conditions prevail in what I will call (without apology) the Grand Passion. It is an intense, almost transcendental

176

experience, with its own dynamic, and it cannot last a long time. It is not love to make a marriage, it is love to make a breakthrough, which acts, as it turns out, to prepare the way for all other love to follow, under whatever conditions life dictates.

She is liable to be someone he has passionately admired from a distance, but with whom he never expected to be intimate. In secret he has projected onto her every human virtue imaginable. He has been extremely careful and correct in his dealings with her, as if she were from some rare, exotic species and might spook at any moment. Above all, he respects her. She is a person of character, with a unique soul whose temper and resonance he imagines he can feel in the air when she walks into a room. He respects her—perhaps to an unreasonable degree—and may even be a little bit afraid of her.

The Source of Health

Although we sometimes identify sexuality with sexual activity and thus see sexuality as occupying a small and isolated portion of our total living and being, we are foolish to deny our functioning as sexual beings. Through an understanding of the full range of love as described by C.S. Lewis (*agape, eros, storge, filia*—divine love, passion, affection, and friendship, respectively), we understand the place of sexual activity and the source of sexual energy, which permeates our entire life.

Creativity and health flow from sexual energy.

Task Force on Human Sexuality and Family Life, *Harper's Magazine*, August 1988.

They have seen each other off and on for many years at various social occasions. Since each is caught up in his own life, and the lives do not overlap in any significant way, they would not appear to have much in common. Thus they are taken by surprise, entering into an experience they hadn't planned for. It is *trouvé*, which lends it a certain purity and authority. A Grand Passion, by its very nature, is not arranged for, it simply happens.

Outside of the World

Over weeks or months they become friends. He continues to control his desire to make love to her, feeling privileged to share her company. He responds instantly, however, when she surprises him with a sign. She wants him.

She is his goddess. We can laugh at him for that, but from his point of view it is absolutely true. . . .

When their union is complete it is as if, paradoxically, they have left their bodies. They sail, they ghost along incorporeal through space, aware of each other's spiritual company, alone together in some indescribable vastness.

He hears something. A dog barking outside, perhaps.

"The world starts up again," she says. "Like a switch." They lie together in each other's arms. They've come back.

Earned Knowledge

If the boy is blinded by the force of his desire, and the young man does not think because he believes the whole thing to be lucky magic, the man begins to see and think. The Grand Passion goes on for months, perhaps years, and relatively simple ideas, which had before been only words, words he understood too easily, become earned knowledge.

To begin with, he deals with the implications of the fact that the woman truly loves him. There was no reason for her to become involved with him, probably plenty of reasons for her not to. She is not *trying* to love him—because she is supposed to love him, or wants to love him, or imagines she loves him. Everything she does and says shows clearly that she *can't help* loving him. He did not create the situation, nor did he seduce her. She flat out loves him, for her own reasons, and that means that the engine that drives her is much the same as the engine that drives him. They are in it together, natural companions under a force that exists, as it were, above them.

The honesty prevailing between them allows him to learn swiftly. His imagination moves past the boundaries of his self-preoccupation. They both know their affair will end eventually, and she, no less than he, has no reason to do the sort of wishful thinking, editing, coloring, and withholding that can mark the exchanges of two people beginning to construct or endeavoring to maintain an edifice expected to last a very long time through God knows what conditions. There is a lack of defensiveness, a lack of fearfulness, and she gives the best answers she can to any questions he asks. She will tell him about her body, her sexuality, her image of herself—indeed, anything he wants to know. There are no secrets. From hundreds of bits, some large and some small, he begins to form a sharper picture both of her and of womankind. To some extent he feels like a visitor returning to a strange country, only this time with a guide who explains that he didn't quite get it before. This is not the mating dance, nor a game, however serious. This is straight. The greatest degree of honesty of which they are capable. He learns who she is, and on the way he learns about himself. He sees himself through her eyes and discovers what is important to her in him, and what is not.

Seeing Clearly

Why does it take so long? One would think that given the amount of time and energy men devote to women they would know them quite well. But for most it is a long journey. A man's need for women distorts his perception of them. He projects his created images onto them, and they are often adept at allowing him to believe they really are those images. Further, men so often bring to bear hidden agendas of which they are genuinely unaware. They become involved with a woman in order to launch themselves into a new stage of life, or to live up to expectations, or to avoid loneliness, or a dozen other perfectly understandable reasons. Men are too fragile and too involved to see women clearly without a woman's help. There is more than one way for the scales to fall from a man's eyes, but the spontaneous, honest, generous, passionate love of a strong woman is perhaps the fastest.

*"Celibacy may be a way of gaining more
control of your life."*

Celibacy Can Improve Relationships

Mitchell Ditkoff

The following viewpoint is the story of a man who chose to remain celibate for five years. Mitchell Ditkoff, a free-lance author,
writes that sex had become less fulfilling and was hindering his
relationships with women. Ditkoff believes his period of celibacy
improved his friendships and gave him more control over his life.

As you read, consider the following questions:

1. Why did Ditkoff become celibate?
2. According to the author, what are the benefits of celibacy?
3. Why did Ditkoff end his period of celibacy?

Mitchell Ditkoff, "I Gave Up Sex for Five Years," *Glamour*, March 1986. Courtesy
Glamour, copyright © 1986 by The Condé Nast Publications, Inc.

As a young man I wanted to be many different things when I grew up. Celibate was not one of them. The very word made me think of shrunken men in single beds, of cold stone floors and of gruel. Where I came from, kids weren't raised to renounce, but to consume. To buy. To get. Sex was simply another commodity, and the more you got, the better off you were. If you had told me then that I'd turn my back on sex one day, I would have laughed in your face. Yet, at the age of thirty, that's just what I did.

Why? Part of me, no doubt, was reacting to a failed marriage. My Romeo dreams of living happily ever after had been shattered, and I was in no mood for trying to revive them. And part of me was influenced by my readings in Eastern philosophy, which advised against intercourse as a needless waste of energy—especially if one were at all interested in "truth."

I'd been popular enough with women in my youth, but more often than not I came away from sexual encounters feeling dissatisfied. No matter how warm and giving my lovers had been, there was always a place inside me I could never allow them to touch.

Two problems seemed to contribute to that dissatisfaction: To begin with, I usually felt these women were so lost in their fantasy of what a lover should be that they weren't making contact with who I really was. In addition, I was forever putting *them* on pedestals in a parallel attempt to have the women I loved be "worthy" of my attention.

Bound To Pitch Forever

Not surprisingly, my relationships didn't work. Again and again I found myself in strange beds, staring at the ceiling and thinking, "This is it?"

Even when sex was good, it was only a matter of time before I turned my lovers into scapegoats for my own unwillingness to get on with what I believed to be more important—finding myself.

The more I blamed my lovers for distracting me from my "higher" goal, the more I saw that *I* was the one with the problem. I was *afraid* of emotion. I was *afraid* of desire. I was afraid of ending up out of control and helplessly subject to the same petty dramas that plagued almost everyone I knew.

Eventually I realized that I actually had a choice about sex; it was perfectly fine to back off and give myself some breathing room. After all, weren't human beings the only species capable of choosing *not* to have sex? Sure, my desire for sex was strong. But so was my desire to pitch for the Dodgers. Did that mean that I was forever bound to throw tennis balls against aluminum garage doors?

Living in an experimental subculture of the 1970's, I also had the chance to observe several men I knew who had recently

"I'm very fond of you, so sex
wouldn't come into it."

become celibate and lived together. For them, sex wasn't much of an issue anymore. Although I questioned them endlessly to satisfy my cynical curiosity about their arrangement, all I found was a sincere desire to create an environment for nurturing personal growth.

Gradually, I began to see that it wasn't a piece of ass that I wanted—it was peace of mind. If I didn't get intimate with myself, my chances of ever getting intimate with anyone else were slim indeed.

My eventual decision to "go celibate" wasn't triggered by a single event. In fact, it was less a decision than a recognition of something that had begun years ago. Somewhere in the back of my mind I'd always sensed that each relationship existed only as a kind of bon voyage party preceding an inevitably lonely journey of self-discovery. I never had any idea how long this journey would take. I just knew that it had to happen.

And so, unable to stall any longer what seemed to be destiny, I took a formal step forward into the unknown. I moved in with my celibate friends.

Thinking Celibate

At first, my celibacy was pure delight. Finally, no need to perform! Finally, no need to prove myself male! And finally, no more hidden agendas! For the first time since I was thirteen, I wasn't approaching women with the secret desire of *getting* something.

Refreshing as this was, I still found myself at the mercy of what seemed like a lifetime of sexual momentum. *Being* celibate and *thinking* celibate, I discovered, were not the same thing. Images of women constantly filled my head. At times, it felt as if my withdrawal from sex had tripped some primal warning system encoded in my cells to protect the race from extinction.

And yet, despite the odds (and how odd I felt), *something* kept me going. I had promised myself to try celibacy, and come hell or wet dreams I was going to.

My primal needs weren't the only obstacles. Everywhere I looked—magazines, billboards, commercials—sylph-like beauties offered to improve my life if only I bought what they were selling, if only I chose to associate my brand of toothpaste with the increased possibility of getting kissed. I learned to tune out these sexual cues.

Time for Self-Development

But I didn't eliminate women from my life. Far from it. I had more women friends than ever before. And, as the variety of my women friends increased, so did the quality of our communication. Since I no longer needed (or expected) sex from them, I could abstain from the mating game rituals most men are weaned on. I could be more honest and direct. No longer ruled by my genitals, I not only listened more, I *wanted* to listen more. In return, these women were glad to relate to a person instead of a potential bedmate. The women who were already familiar with my personal drama over the past few years required no explanations. For the others, my celibacy was usually no more of an issue than which football team I rooted for or what kind of music I liked.

As the emotional drama drained from my life, I found the time for other avenues of self-development. My need for companionship and physical pleasure? What I once thought likely to come only from a lover I now experienced in other ways—through yoga and meditation, an expanding network of friends and a willingness to take one day at a time.

The more I trusted my celibacy, the better I felt. It became easier to see how I had been tyrannized for years by my compulsion to always have a lover. Ever since I'd learned about Noah's Ark, I'd thought that survival in this world meant going "two by two." Well, I was going alone, and it felt good.

Ann Landers's Rule

I am in a [celibate] relationship now. It's a switch for me, too: a decision made after examining the practical implications of morality, old and new, and realizing we would all probably be a lot better off if we followed Ann Landers's rule of courtship: between the two of you, keep three feet on the ground at all times. . . .The restraint we are practicing now is the foundation for a parallel partnership that respects independence.

Ginger Lyon, *Southline*, May 4, 1988.

More women seemed attracted to me at this time (perhaps since my attitude was no longer predatory). So, while some of my critics were assuming my celibacy was involuntary, I knew otherwise. It was my choice, and in some ways, I had chosen it with a greater passion than I had chosen any relationship. Since there were few role models in this area to compete with, I also felt my choice to be celibate was freer than most choices I'd made in my life. Knowing that I had the option to end it gave me boundless energy to take it still further. I experienced the well-being I imagine dieters feel, knowing there's food in the fridge but having the will not to raid it.

Taking a Chance Again

The pieces of my life were integrating in a way I'd never thought possible. I felt expansive, excited and more open to love than ever. One thing was becoming clear: I did long for a special kind of intimacy. Unlike most unmarried men my age, my quest was not to find my "other half"—rather, it was to find what was *whole* about me. I wanted to discover who I was, apart from all roles and relationships. To my mother, I was a son. To my sister, I was a brother. To my ex-wife, I was an ex-husband. But to myself? Who was I then? Paradoxically, I could only play the role of a man once I learned I was much more than that role.

After five years of sleeping alone, I began to sense the old familiar feeling that had always preceded the end of my intimate relationships—the one that signaled "It's over." Now, however, what was ending was my relationship to *not* having a relationship. I finally felt safe enough to take a chance with a woman once again. It was time to say "yes" to life instead of "Later, I'm busy searching for the Truth."

And Diana was the right one to say yes to. Just being near her was a welcome assault on my senses. I wanted to deny my desire—but I knew I couldn't. The jig was up.

It wasn't that Diana was perfect for me; the timing was right for both of us. Here was a woman who offered simply a hearty transition back to a life of learning through love.

The Right Decision

I bit more than a few bullets trying to decide whether making love again would somehow neutralize the five years I'd invested in my search for self. Would I later bemoan my lack of self-discipline?

Sitting next to Diana on her living room couch dwarfed all my questions. I simply felt too much love to analyze the situation. A month before, perhaps, it would have been enough just to listen to her story: the ex-husband, the kid, the lack of good men in her life. But this was now. And I was glad. It mattered little that I felt nervous. I was about to make love to a woman I liked, and that felt better than ever.

Diana and I saw each other for about six months after that. Our relationship taught me more, I think, about letting go of old expectations and roles than the previous five years of meditation. I spoke to her on the phone a month ago, and she seems happier than ever.

Recently, Barbara, an old friend of mine, told me she'd once been celibate for seven years but hadn't enjoyed it. She went on to say that a lot of people she knew, because of demands of career and family life, or the shortage of suitable companions, had also experienced extended periods of celibacy. Most of these people, explained Barbara, never accepted their sexual inactivity. On the contrary, they perceived it as an embarrassment—something to end, not something to understand.

In retrospect, I can see that a lot of people I met along the way didn't understand my celibacy, either. Most of them were spooked by it. And many of those who deliberately tried it didn't take it far enough to learn from the experience.

I don't know why people think that sleeping with someone else will solve all their problems. It would be great if it did. But it doesn't. While making love certainly can provide some of the most blissful moments on earth, it still can't substitute for the need we all have to know our own selves better.

Celibacy may be a way of gaining more control of your life. It may even be the medium through which you discover who you are when there's no one around to tell you.

"Having sex makes you feel good, and increasing your erotic sophistication improves your self-esteem."

Sexual Experimentation Makes Relationships More Exciting

Even Eve

The Kerista Village is a commune in which members are not monogamous. They practice polyfidelity—they have sex with other members of their group, but not with outsiders. In the following viewpoint, Even Eve, a member of the commune since 1971, explains that such sexual experimentation increases creativity and happiness.

As you read, consider the following questions:

1. According to the author, what are the benefits of sexual experimentation?
2. Why do people resist sexual experimentation, according to the author?
3. What does the author believe will be the results of sexual experimentation?

Even Eve, "The Erotic Evolution of Kerista," *Kerista*, Winter 1987. Reprinted with permission.

There was a period of time when an article in *Psychology Today* featuring Kerista as a rare and unusual example of non-monogamous people who were jealousy-free prompted TV talk show producers across the nation to contact us and invite us to appear on their shows. We did the *Phil Donahue Show*, the *Today Show* and a number of appearances on local (San Francisco Bay Area) programs. By the eighth or ninth show, we were feeling sort of burned out on describing our sleeping schedule to middle America and thought it would make a lot of sense to start focusing the discussions more on other elements of our lifestyle, like our plan to create a grassroots philanthropic movement that could solve serious world problems. No go. The dialogue always came back to what Phil Donahue called "the sex part" of the trip and stayed there, regardless of efforts to shoot off in other directions.

A Natural Preoccupation with Sex

I see this as a plus, really. At least there's *something* that gets people's attention. When I first came into contact with Kerista and Keristans—of whom, at the time, there were only a handful—one of the first things I heard was the maxim, "It all boils down to penises and vaginas." Though I had been moving in hip circles, I was startled by such a blunt reduction of all life's complicated mysteries. Yet it seemed, on reflection, to be fairly accurate, even if hyperbolically stated. My main preoccupation back then was certainly sex-related. What type of relationship, or relationships, did I want? How many? Sex with women and men or men only? And what about all those stereotypical sex roles? How should I get rid of them, and who could I meet that would agree with me about them? Was it true that the vaginal orgasm was a myth? Was there really such a thing as a happy couple? And on and on, ad nauseam at times.

Life in Kerista clarified the significance of the boiling it all down to genitals homily. It wasn't that other things weren't important or wonderful. It was just, very simply, that until a person had sorted all those issues out and gotten her/his intimate life into a satisfactory place, everything else was to some degree put on hold. First things first. My guess about most people is that a lot of this sort-and-find stuff related to their sex lives goes on subliminally, without much consciousness, because it's only very recently that sexual matters have begun coming up to the surface for open thought and discussion. This means that an awful lot of people are going around with a good portion of their total awareness potential buried, as it were, in underground vaults where they can't do much with it. Just imagine what the world could be like if that locked up potential was liberated for conscious, intelligent use! Despite periodic societal regressions, I think things are going that way. . . .

The idea of polyfidelity has immense erotic appeal to those of us who've opted for it for reasons beyond the sexual fact of sleeping with a number of wonderful partners. One of the biggest draws is the erotic relationship between the people of the same sex who (in hetero groups such as those existing in Kerista) share the experience of relating sexually to the same opposite sex people. We call these people "starling" sisters or brothers, and these friendships are unique and delightful. There has been a lively debate going on within the commune for several years now connected to this, having to do with trust and closeness. According to those on one side of the debate, there are two "tiers" of relationships in a B-FIC [Best Friend Identity Cluster], with two different levels of closeness. In the closest tier or ring are the sexual relationships; in the second ring are the starlings. Both are precious, but (according to this perspective) sexual relations have innately more depth of feeling, trust and intimacy than platonics. On the other side of the debate is the view that there is no inherent difference in trust and closeness between sexual and platonic B-FIC relationships. The two types of involvements are different but equal; the determinants of how intimate you are with any of your partners has to do with other factors, such as how long you've been together and what sorts of shared experiences you've logged in. According to this second theory, in fact, you might feel closer to a same-sex, platonic partner with whom you've had a stable friendship for many years than to a sexual partner who has only come into the group recently, and has had a history of being unstable in B-FICs due to unsettled psychological issues.

Revealing Secrets

In sleeping with a number of lovers, secrets are revealed that otherwise remain shrouded—such as the infinite mysteries of sexual technique. . . . Milan Kundera wrote of this in *The Unbearable Lightness of Being*: "Isn't making love merely an eternal repetition of the same? Not at all. There is always the small part that is unimaginable."

David Talbot, *Utne Reader*, June/July 1986.

This is the kind of dialectical debate that we find very enjoyable, and pursue in a relaxed and leisurely fashion as we drift through life with each other, without the expectation that one side will ever convince the other to change their views. Conversations about themes like this presuppose a high degree of erotic sophistication. We do not deal with any jealousy whatsoever and never have within the Keristan life-style. But there *are* things that have taken some working out. I can remember the time, about nine or ten years ago, that Lee and Jud decided to go out to see a live sex show at one of the adult theaters in San Francisco. This was shortly after we had all decided to let go of most of our former erotic restrictions. They came in late that night, having had a good time, and some of us asked them to describe the show. After hearing a brief description, I made a face and said something like, "I don't know *how* you could find watching women masturbate entertaining," in my snottiest tone of voice. Lee looked at me and said, "Well Mr. Jones, how long have you been beating your wife?" At that point I backed down from my implied superiority position and began to realize that the amount of emotionality I was feeling probably had very little to do with the immediate situation and was something I'd really have to take a good look at.

That process of self-examination and sexual attitude restructuring took me and everyone else years—in fact, we're still in it today. It may seem surprising that people who had already progressed so far from their cultural roots and embraced the ideal of social tolerance so sincerely would be uncovering layers of erotic prejudice in themselves. On the other hand, it only underscores the fact that faulty conditioning and education can and do have a big impact on people's minds.

Resisting Change

I used to be very puzzled by my own and others' initial emotional response to the introduction of new ideas for pushing out our boundaries of erotic exploration. Really, none of the things we've examined or tried have even been all that far out, compared to other things I'm aware of. According to friends and acquaintances, Keristans are still into what's known as "vanilla sex." But we have explored such ideas as setting up a very select club called the "Perfect Partners Co-op Cabaret" which would be a place where exhibitionists within our social circle could perform before a sympathetic audience, and we've dabbled in consensual, intellectual erotic games wherein different people will take on dominant or submissive roles, and the submissives will carry out instructions given by the dominants. These instructions have actually been non-sexual for the most part, and are designed to help the person playing the submissive role develop her/himself in areas that can use improvement.

But back to the puzzlement. I've had the sense that there was something more to the nervous or fearful response than simply the echo of juvenile conditioning. What I've finally concluded is that it's basic mental inertia; the resistance to change. This is one of the funnier aspects of human nature, but a real one we have to contend with. I've noticed something very interesting about people when they have some kind of new sexual or erotic experience. Almost without exception, it seems to step up their self-confidence by at least a tiny bit, and sometimes by a lot. And sometimes, along with that, there seems to be a little more looseness, a little more creativity.

I'm not just talking about the fact that getting laid cheers people up. That is something I've observed so often that I don't even question it anymore. To whatever degree I might have doubted it, my doubts were finally eradicated when I was in a period of recovering from a long and serious depression. I wasn't totally depressed anymore, but I still had attacks of it that would sometimes last for days. One day when I was feeling pretty bad I came into the front room of one of our houses, where Jaz and Ram, two men in my B-FIC, were hanging out. Ram, who was filling out his workslips for the day, saw that I was in a low mood. . . . "Why don't you two go into the Pink Room and have yourselves a freebie! At least one of you'll enjoy it, anyway," [he said.] So Jaz and I followed his advice. When we started fooling around I was still feeling so bad I was crying a little. Midway through the cunnilingus, before I even came, my mood switched. By the time we finished I was feeling 100% better. This wasn't a one-time phenomenon—I tested it numerous other times (purely in the interest of scientific research, of course) and found it worked repeatedly. Sex gets your endorphins flowing, the chemicals in your brain that make you feel good.

Bringing Out the Best

Sexual experimentation . . . often brings out the best in me. Living life this fully, of course, can be massively self-indulgent. But it also demands a level of empathy, consideration and imagination toward which we should all aspire.

David Talbot, *Utne Reader*, June/July 1986.

Having sex makes you feel good, and increasing your erotic sophistication improves your self-esteem. These aren't absolutes—sex in a relationship that's already burned out might not do much for you (although many a burned out relationship will hang together for years based on the sex alone)—but I think these are generalizations that will hold up. Erotic self-development increases self-esteem because it involves the use of the mind; it expands the imagination; it makes you feel modern, up-to-date, gives you a glamorous self-image. Because it involves an intellectual workout, you may run into a wall of inertia that wants you to stay put as you are, the same way you may suddenly feel very sedentary when someone invites you to go for a jog. But just as habitual joggers know that on the other side of the inertia are a number of personal rewards, people who choose to see themselves as erotically sophisticated and are willing to look for and engage those new ideas will reap benefits of their own: the benefits of sexual liberation. The two (sexual liberation and erotic sophistication) come together, if you will; they're a package deal. . . .

Of all the things Keristans are trying to do, the most urgent and important is our plan to create a broad-based megacommune network that will function as a civilian branch of service and generate huge amounts of philanthropic funding that will be used to solve global problems. It is the most urgent and important thing because the welfare of humanity and our planet may be at stake if our plan—or *some* plan, and we don't know of any others—fails to work. But my guess is that the way we're going to get people to join us and help us make the plan succeed will be by appealing to them on the basis of the things that really hit home, no matter how stone cold intellectual they may be: sex and eroticism. The world will be liberated from the yoke of economic oppression and ecological suicide through sex. How's that for a hippie concept? It's twenty years since the Summer of Love, and the spirit of the Haight-Ashbury lives on.

"For those adventurers who can make the leap into commitment, the rewards are great."

Monogamy Is Rewarding

George Leonard

"No, romance doesn't fade. It changes color." So spoke a happily married woman in her mid-forties. Her sincerity inspired George Leonard, a former editor of *Look* magazine who was writing a book called *Future Sex*, to retitle his work *Adventures in Monogamy*. As he interviewed others he became convinced that monogamy was more challenging, but also more rewarding, than its alternatives. The following viewpoint is an excerpt from his book.

As you read, consider the following questions:

1. What does the author mean by the phrase High Monogamy?
2. What, according to Leonard, are the virtues needed for High Monogamy?
3. What does Leonard claim are the rewards of High Monogamy?

High monogamy . . . [is] a long-term relationship in which both members are *voluntarily* committed to erotic exclusivity, not because of legal, moral or religious scruples, not because of timidity or inertia, *but because they seek challenge and an adventure.*

High Monogamy requires, first of all, a goodly supply of self-esteem in both partners. Psychologist Nathaniel Branden, one of the rare modern writers who advocates romantic love, argues that no other factor is more important.

> It has become something of a cliché to observe that, if we do not love ourselves, we cannot love anyone else. This is true enough, but it is only part of the picture. If we do not love ourselves, it is almost impossible to believe fully that we *are loved* by someone else. It is almost impossible to *accept* love. It is almost impossible to *receive* love. No matter what our partner does to show that he or she cares, we do not experience the devotion as convincing because we do not feel lovable to ourselves.

Self-esteem, no matter how important, is not all that is required of those who would take the path of High Monogamy. It is essential that both partners have mutual interests and share a common vision of life's purpose and how to achieve it. Each partner needs the ability to celebrate and support the other, not only in low moments but also in high. "Never marry a person," Nathaniel Branden tells his clients, "who is not a friend of your excitement." The High Monogamist is not blindly approving but rather is dedicated to an uncommon openness and honesty. At the same time, he or she knows *how* to be open and honest without being abrasive or dogmatic.

The Necessary Virtues

Some of the virtues needed for High Monogamy—such things as enthusiasm, loyalty, courtesy, and patience—have become so platitudinous as to fade into the background noise of the modern world. And yet, unacknowledged, their presence or absence shapes the outcome of every relationship. In a book on marriage, the great psychologist Carl Rogers tells us that when he turned forty he mysteriously became impotent. This condition lasted a year, during which his wife remained cheerful, loving, and supportive. At the end of the year, his impotence disappeared, never to return. His wife's uncanny patience so touched Rogers that he knew he would love her until the end of her days.

Still, it is not merely the exercise of the common virtues that marks the High Monogamist, but rather a sort of towering, vertiginous daring. For this state requires that we look directly and unflinchingly at our every weakness and flaw, straight down through layer after layer of cowardice and self-deception to the very heart of our intentionality. And in High Monogamy we are forced, as well, to confront something even more terrifying: our beauty and magnificence, our potential to love and create and feel deeply, and the daily, hourly, moment-by-moment waste of that potential. And when we achieve the unnerving clarity that High Monogamy demands, we must either beat a fast retreat or undertake to transform ourselves.

The New Pragmatism

The new bywords are commitment and responsibility. . . . Maybe it's the eternal dream of true love or possibly just a new pragmatism. Sexual freedom doesn't seem quite so appealing in the age of AIDS.

Barbara Kantrowitz, *Newsweek*, August 24, 1987.

Simone de Beauvoir has argued that eroticism "is a movement toward the *Other*, this is its essential character, but in the deep intimacy of the couple, husband and wife become for one another the *Same*; no exchange is any longer possible, no giving and no conquering." De Beauvoir in this case failed to look deeply enough into the possibilities of the monogamous situation. High Monogamy is not a mere fusion, not a mutual loss of self. It is the reassertion of a more fundamental self, explainable only through paradox: *The more I am truly myself, the more I can be truly one with you. The more I am truly one with you, the more I can be truly myself.* The paradox is inescapable. In High Monogamy, the couple constitutes a single entity made of two autonomous entities. For each person, the partner is both the Same *and* the Other. In this regard, the couple models the ancient mystery of multiplicity within unity, identity within holonomy.

Sexual Stasis

It is easy to associate multiple sexual partners with personal change and monogamy with personal stasis. This can at times be true; after years of the stultification of what might be called Low Monogamy, having an affair can reawaken dulled perceptions and trigger a transformation of sorts. But extramarital affairs or the pursuit of recreational sex are far more likely to be associated with the avoidance of change. After superficial erotic novelty has faded, after ego has had its full run (all the life stories told, all the sexual tricks displayed), *then* the adventure of transformation and a deeper eroticism can begin. But it is precisely at this point that most of us are likely to lose our nerve and leap into another bed, where we can once again tell our stories, display our tricks, do *anything* rather than see ourselves clearly and start doing something about it.

Indeed, one glimpse into the powerful mirror of High Monogamy might be all it takes to send us back into the desolate comfort of Low Monogamy or out in hot pursuit of the-same-thing-another-time-around. In either case, the underlying, unacknowledged aim is to avoid change, to be allowed to lead an essentially predictable life. High Monogamy, merciless in its presentation of self-knowledge, demands that we change, that we have the courage to lead an essentially unpredictable life.

Advocates of multiple sex have a saying: "Why should I be satisfied with a sandwich when there's a feast out there?" Obviously, they have never experienced High Monogamy. Those of us who have tried both tend to see it differently. Casual recreational sex is hardly a feast—not even a good, hearty sandwich. It is a diet of fast food served in plastic containers. Life's feast is available only to those who are willing and able to engage life on a deeply personal level, giving all, holding back nothing.

Leap into Commitment

It would be a mistake to overpraise High Monogamy. Nothing is quite as glorious as it can be made to sound, and human beings are ingenious in discovering ways to sabotage their own joy. Still, for those adventurers who can make the leap into commitment, the rewards are great: a rare tenderness, an exaltation, a highly charged erotic ambience, surprise on a daily basis, transformation. But there is no insurance policy.

No wonder High Monogamy is so rare and so rarely even mentioned. The survey takers, in fact, suggest that it is virtually impossible. Romance fades, they proclaim, after an average of fifteen months. Or is it eighteen months, or three years? In any case, romance fades. And they are often right. Civilization has trained us well in restlessness and manipulation. To be prepared for civilization's work of building and doing, of conquest and exploitation, it is best to be somewhat uneasy in our skins, dissatisfied with the present moment. Romance seems merely palliative. Dis-ease is habitual. We fall out of the present. We forget our lover is the universe. Glancing anxiously at the past and the future, we resort to calculation. Our lover becomes, again, an object, an *It*. Ignoring our heart's desire, we conclude the survey takers are right. For most of us, High Monogamy remains a condition to be realized, difficult to describe, much less achieve. Its converse is easy, [according to Simone de Beauvoir]:

> We dedicate ourselves to job, school, politics, golf. We let love take care of itself. What happens? A joining that begins in passion relapses into cliché while the first fresh taste of love is still on your lips. The moment comes (too soon!) when you run across tax forms among old love letters. "Notice of Adjustment. Part I—Tax-Payer's Copy." And suddenly, Sunday finds you sprawled not on that high, singing meadow where the eyes of your love were able somehow to hold the universe but in front of the TV. After six hours of pro football, the most brilliantly executed fake

buck and roll-out seems trivial; the beer tastes like used detergent; the peanuts lie like hot mud at the bottom of your belly. Your love walks by, and a mechanical hand (one of yours?) reaches up to pat her on the fanny. As for her, she shakes her head and moves to check the washing machine. The machine churns in the background. Everything is secure. But your love isn't there. Her mind has flown her to that faraway sea of poppies on the edge of the cornfield where she is saying over and over, as did Madame Bovary, "O God, O God, why did I get married?"

And yet the dream persists. We look at those rare couples who are still mad for each other after twenty years of marriage, who embarrass us with their dinner party embraces, as somehow freakish, exceptions who prove the rule. Still, we envy them. In spite of surveys, hard experience and Sexual Revolution dogma, we launch ourselves again and again toward surrender and commitment. Some subterranean impulse draws us into romance even when it is unfashionable.

True Love

The cynic's wisdom has a long pedigree. Perhaps we would be wise to settle for healthy sensuality, recreational sex. . . . Commitment is scary. Perceiving our lover as the universe can lead to unrealistic expectations and thus to hurt and disillusionment. So we may choose to be "realistic" to lower our expectations, to go on making the sort of half-hearted, calculated commitment that so often leads to Skinnerian entrapment, then to infidelity or open marriage. Or maybe we're willing, from the beginning, to settle for creature comforts, parallel play, companionate love. Maybe it is irresponsible to push anyone toward the terrors of total commitment.

===

Safe and Cozy

The monogamous no longer contemplate the unattached and agonize over lost freedom. When monogamy is seen as safe and cozy, the sexual mini-dramas coming out of the single life just aren't as titillating as they used to be.

Arising out of that appreciation for monogamy is a willingness to work harder at maintaining a relationship.

Peter Mehlman, *Glamour*, July 1988.

===

But there is also something terrifying about the waste of potential. This life is as sharp as the edge of a sword between an eternity behind us and an eternity ahead. Perhaps the cut is clean and true only when, on certain fine occasions, we give all of ourselves, relinquishing all expectations, judgement, and considered opinion, living bravely in the eternal moment. We cannot make that cut through abstraction, generalization, classification, and categorization—those sometimes-useful tools of civilization are the enemies of love and creation—but only through a repersonalization of all of life. Habits can take weeks, months, or years to turn around, but perceptions can change in an instant. New perceptions are prerequisite for all significant change, providing both guidance and impetus for the process of transformation that follows.

Dangerous Destiny

We begin, as I have said, by seeing the human individual as a vibrant and unique field of energy, as a window into the universe, even as the universe itself. This radical repersonalization is by no means the exclusive prerogative of those who are dedicated to High Monogamy, who are fortunate enough to have found their longtime mates. It is also possible, as I've suggested, in an erotic encounter that lasts only a few brief hours. All truly erotic love involves two vibrant entities merging to become a new vibrancy, something truly novel in the universe. And when love ends, something of that vibrancy remains, some enrichment of all of existence.

No act of love is intrinsically trivial. We have been carefully taught in countless covert ways to make it so. But at every instant a choice remains: to perceive anew, to brush the cobwebs of custom from our eyes, to surrender to the dangerous destiny of truly personal love.

"Like many other species, humans have a strong urge for variety in sexual partners."

Monogamy Is Stifling

Jules Older

Jules Older is a clinical psychologist in Orleans, Vermont. In the following viewpoint, he argues that monogamy is not natural for people. Older contends that human promiscuity is biologically determined. Therefore, people should not be judged harshly if they cannot remain monogamous.

As you read, consider the following questions:

1. According to the author, what biological factor makes the human species promiscuous?
2. What proof does Older offer that promiscuity is inherent in humans?
3. Why does Older object to enforced monogamy?

Jules Older, "Mother Nature's Dirty Trick," *Los Angeles Times*, March 12, 1988. Reprinted with permission.

When the news broke that the Rev. Marvin Gorman had caught the Rev. Jimmy Swaggart with a prostitute, one word came to just about everybody's mind: hypocrisy. The scourge of promiscuous preachers, the man who'd accused Gorman of adultery and helped bring down Jim Bakker on the same charge, had been caught with his own britches down. To make matters worse, it turned out that Swaggart has a history of extramarital dalliances.

But Swaggart's apparent hypocrisy isn't all that unusual. As a society—perhaps as a species—we succeed rather well in pretending to be something we aren't. Although we drape ourselves in the white cloak of monogamy, we know—and try hard to deny—that *homo sapiens* is a promiscuous species.

Our Secret Vice

We go to some trouble to say it isn't so. We pass laws against adultery, pay preachers to denounce promiscuity and profess to be shocked when, time after time, upright citizens are found to be running around. Promiscuity is our secret vice and the source of our greatest hypocrisy.

We acknowledge that chimps and dogs are anything but monogamous. We know that gorillas and elephant seals are polygynous. We accept that they are the way they are because their behavior is biologically built-in. But most of us won't accept that *homo sapiens* carry similar built-ins. We take them to school, to the office and yea, verily, even unto the pulpit on Sunday morning.

Attraction to Strangers

And all the time we're carrying this evolutionary load in our genes, we swear that we're not. We hate to admit that, like many other species, humans have a strong urge for variety in sexual partners. Our condition is summed up in the ancient Arab proverb, "The newcomer filleth the eye."

I call this condition xenerotica, meaning sexual attraction to strangers. I believe that it's built into human behavior.

The evidence?

Let's start with the Revs. Swaggart, Gorman and Bakker, and for good measure throw in another famous evangelist, Aimee Semple McPherson. All gained fame and fortune from their ability to denounce sin in entertaining ways. Topping their long list of sins were sins of the flesh. Yet each of these preachers risked shame and infamy—not to mention eternity in hell—for sexual variety. And all got caught.

But these are individual cases; where is the evidence that a need for sexual variety is inherent in the rest of us? Let's start with a look at the way we're built.

Humans are a moderately dimorphic species, meaning that the

physical differences between the sexes are fairly pronounced. Male humans are 8% taller and 20% heavier than females. What's more, among primates, the human male's genitals are exceptionally large, and no other primate has mammaries as conspicuous as the human female's.

Dimorphism tells a lot about sexual habits. Species with only slight differences in size and appearance between males and females tend to be strictly monogamous. The gibbon is a good example, and it seems to mate for life. By contrast, species that are highly dimorphic, such as gorillas and elephant seals, are highly polygynous. The 3-ton male southern elephant seal keeps a harem stocked with as many as 48 mates.

dredge

*"Bloody marvellous how our marriage
has lasted all these years, Gladys!"*

Our moderate dimorphism is nature's joke on us. It means we are forever locked into conflict between monogamous and promiscuous urges. No matter how tightly we're bonded to a mate, the newcomer will still filleth the eye.

More support for xenerotica comes from studies of human behavior. In the late 1940s and early '50s, researcher Alfred Kinsey outraged decent Americans by revealing that they engaged in a lot more sexual activity than they admitted. A 1970s update by Morton Hunt showed that Kinsey's findings were no fluke. Indeed, Hunt found that sexual activity, in and out of marriage, had significantly increased since the Kinsey Report, particularly among women.

A 1983 survey of 100,000 *Playboy* readers refuted the notion that those who seek sexual variety do so because of sexual dissatisfaction at home: "Our figures suggest that by the age of 50, almost 70% of men and 65% of women have had an affair. Women who say they are sexually satisfied are less likely to cheat; for men, it doesn't matter. No matter what they think of their sex lives, men fool around."

Two studies reported in 1988—one by eight evangelical church denominations, the other by the Pentagon—showed that 43% of teen-agers attending conservative churches have had sexual intercourse by their 18th birthday. That's almost the percentage of pregnant unmarried women in the Navy.

Brought Down by Hypocrisy

Further evidence of xenerotica comes from what we read. *Playboy* and *Penthouse* are the best-selling men's magazines in the world. And, while the relatively sexless *Sports Illustrated* sells 130,000 copies from newsstands in the average week, its annual swimsuit issue sells 1½ million, largely for what the swimsuits reveal. Dr. Dora Lee Dauma, past president of the Central New York chapter of the National Organization for Women, commented, "When it comes to swimsuits, I'm not sure there are any mature men."

I rest my case. If we define maturity or goodness or righteousness or mental health by the standard of unflagging monogamous thoughts and behavior, we are swimming against the full tide of a powerful built-in force. If we denounce those who stray from absolute monogamy, we commit the same high hypocrisy as the fallen evangelists. They made fortunes by denouncing sex. But their own xenerotic biology brought them down in the end.

Evaluating Sources of Information

A critical thinker must always question sources of information. Historians, for example, distinguish between *primary sources* (eyewitness accounts) and *secondary sources* (writings or statements based on primary or eyewitness accounts or on other secondary sources). The account of a nineteenth-century Mormon who had several wives is a primary source. An historian evaluating sexual philosophies in America by using the man's account is an example of a secondary source.

To read and think critically, one must be able to recognize primary sources. This is not enough, however, because eyewitness accounts do not always provide accurate descriptions. The man may have exaggerated the benefits of polygamy in order to gain acceptance for a practice which is still illegal in the US. The historian must take such biases into account.

Test your skill in evaluating sources of information by completing the following exercise. Pretend your teacher tells you to write a research paper on sexual philosophies in the wake of the sexual revolution. You decide to include an equal number of primary and secondary sources. Listed below are a number of sources which may be useful for your research. *Place a P next to those descriptions you believe are primary sources.* Then *rank the primary sources* assigning the number (1) to what appears to be the most accurate and fair primary source, the number (2) to the next most accurate, and so on until the ranking is finished. Next, *place an S next to those descriptions you believe are secondary sources and rank them also, using the same criteria.*

If you are doing this activity as a member of a class or group, discuss and compare your evaluation with other members of the group. Others may come to different conclusions than you. Listening to their reasons may give you valuable insights in evaluating sources of information.

P = *primary*
S = *secondary*

_____ 1. The diary of a woman who became sexually active in the early years of the sexual revolution. _____

_____ 2. An article in an historical journal on the root causes of the sexual revolution. _____

_____ 3. A memoir of sexual experimentation in a commune, written by a man who is now a leading figure in the call for sexual liberation. _____

_____ 4. An ABC television news report on the state of marriage. _____

_____ 5. A book entitled, *The New Chastity: Twenty Men and Women Speak Out.* _____

_____ 6. Viewpoint 2 in this chapter. _____

_____ 7. An editorial in *The New York Times* on love and sex in the 1990s. _____

_____ 8. An article in *Reader's Digest* entitled "Six Steps to Better Sex." _____

_____ 9. A report by the National Institutes of Health on the sexual practices of young adults. _____

_____ 10. A transcript of an interview with a famous sex researcher. _____

_____ 11. An American minister's account of the changes he has seen in attitudes toward monogamy. _____

_____ 12. Viewpoint 3 in this chapter. _____

_____ 13. A book entitled *Evangelical Youth and the Search for Purity.* _____

_____ 14. A public television documentary on the return to traditional values. _____

_____ 15. A newspaper story on reactions to media coverage of the return of monogamy. _____

Periodical Bibliography

The following articles have been selected to supplement the diverse views presented in this chapter.

Father Augustine	"Help and Hope for the Sex Addict," *America*, October 1, 1988.
Louise Bernikow	"What Makes a Man Sexy Today," *Cosmopolitan*, December 1987.
Joani Blank	"How To Have Outstanding Outercourse," *Utne Reader*, September/October 1988.
William F. Buckley Jr.	"Where's the Pressure?" *National Review*, January 22, 1988.
Barbara De Angelis	"Seven Truths about Sex," *Reader's Digest*, August 1987.
Barbara Ehrenreich	"Single Jeopardy," *Ms.*, May 1989.
Jean Bethke Elshtain	"What's the Matter with Sex Today?" *Tikkun*, March/April 1988. Available from The Institute for Labor and Mental Health, 5100 Leona St., Oakland, CA 94619.
Brook Hersey	"In Praise of Fly-by-Night Romances," *Glamour*, October 1987.
George Leonard	"In Praise of Monogamy," *American Health*, November 1988.
George Leonard	"The Case for Pleasure," *Esquire*, May 1989.
Ginger Lyon	"(Don't) Do It: A Story of Romantic Restraint," *Utne Reader*, September/October 1988.
Marian Sandmaier	"Sex Shy: Why We're Still Squeamish After All These Years," *Mademoiselle*, April 1989.
Joseph M. Stowell	"Making Marriage Stick," *Moody Monthly*, February 1989.
Peter Trachtenberg	"The Man Who Couldn't Be Faithful," *Mademoiselle*, May 1989.
Walter Wangerin Jr.	"How To Say No to Adultery," *U.S. Catholic*, March 1988.

Organizations To Contact

The editors have compiled the following list of organizations which are concerned with the issues debated in this book. All of them have publications or information available for interested readers. The descriptions are derived from materials provided by the organizations. This list was compiled upon the date of publication. Names and phone numbers of organizations are subject to change.

American Civil Liberties Union (ACLU)
132 W. 43rd St.
New York, NY 10036
(212) 944-9800

The ACLU champions the rights set forth in the Declaration of Independence and the US Constitution. It opposes censorship and supports civil rights for homosexuals. It publishes a monthly newsletter, *First Principles*, and a bimonthly newspaper, *Civil Liberties*.

American Social Health Association (ASHA)
PO Box 13827
Research Triangle Park, NC 27709
(614) 885-4347

ASHA was founded in 1912 to fight against the spread of syphilis and other sexually transmitted diseases. Today it works against AIDS as well, distributing information, operating national hotlines, funding research, and developing educational materials. Its publications include *The Truth About Herpes*, *Questions and Answers About AIDS*, and the quarterly journal, *The Helper*, on the latest research on herpes.

Citizens for Decency Through Law (CDL)
2845 E. Camelback Rd., Suite 740
Phoenix, AZ 85016
(602) 381-1322

CDL is the oldest and largest nonprofit antipornography organization in the US. Its ultimate goal is the total elimination of pornography. CDL consists of a legal and an education department. The legal department provides attorneys who will gather evidence, prepare cases, argue in court, and handle appeals for the prosecution in antipornography cases. The education department provides information on the civil and legal methods by which individuals can combat pornography. CDL distributes many books, including *The Seduction of Society*, *Call to Righteousness*, *Pornography's Victims*, and the monthly newsletter *CDL Reporter*.

Concerned Women for America
370 L'Enfant Promenade SW, Suite 800
Washington, DC 20024
(202) 488-7000

This group works to strengthen the traditional family according to Judeo-Christian moral standards. It publishes several brochures, including *Teen Pregnancy and School-Based Health Clinics*.

The Couple to Couple League (CCL)
3621 Glenmore Ave.
PO Box 111184
Cincinnati, OH 45211-1184
(513) 661-7612

CCL provides education on natural family-planning methods. It supports the institution of marriage and opposes premarital sex. Its publications include *The Art of Natural Family Planning, Marriage—The Mystery of Faithful Love,* and *Sexual Sterilization: Some Questions and Answers.*

Courage
c/o St. Michael's Rectory
424 W. 34th St.
New York, NY 10001
(212) 421-0426

Courage is an organization of homosexuals who wish to live by the teachings of the Roman Catholic Church. It uses support groups and prayers to encourage members to lead celibate lives. It publishes the *Courage Newsletter* quarterly.

Dignity, Inc.
1500 Massachusetts Ave. NW, Suite 11
Washington, DC 20005
(202) 861-0017

Dignity is made up of gay and lesbian members of the Roman Catholic Church who believe that homosexuality and Catholicism are reconcilable. They disagree with the Church's teaching that homosexuals should practice abstinence, believing instead that homosexuals can be sexually active without breaking God's laws. They publish the *Theological Pastoral Resources: A Collection of Articles on Homosexuality from a Catholic Perspective.*

Eagle Forum
PO Box 618
Alton, IL 62002
(618) 462-5415

Eagle Forum is dedicated to preserving traditional family values based on the Bible. It is against premarital sex and sex education. It publishes the *Phyllis Schlafly Report,* a monthly newsletter.

Homosexual Information Center (HIC)
PO Box 8252
Universal City, CA 91608
(318) 742-4709

The Center fights sodomy laws, prostitution statutes, and adult entertainment zoning ordinances. It favors lowering the age of consent for sexual intercourse. HIC publishes an international directory of homosexual organizations and services, as well as *Seeds of the American Sexual Revolution, Prostitution Is Legal, The Lesbian Paperback,* and a bibliography on homosexuality.

Human Life Center
University of Steubenville
Steubenville, OH 43952
(614) 282-9953

The Center teaches natural family planning and conservative Roman Catholic moral values regarding sex, marriage, and family. It publishes two quarterlies, *International Review* and *Human Life Issues.*

INTINET Resource Center
PO Box 2096
Mill Valley, CA 94942

INTINET advocates the "expanded family," a number of adults who are members of a group marriage, who often share food, housing, and child rearing. Sexual relationships between the adults can be of heterosexual or homosexual nature. INTINET distributes information on the expanded family, which it believes will one day be the predominant lifestyle. Publications include *The Expanded Family Network* and *A Resource Guide for the Responsible Non-Monogamist.*

The Lifestyles Organization
2331 W. Sequoia Ave.
Anaheim, CA 92801-3335
(714) 520-4127

The Lifestyles Organization promotes swinging, a practice where married couples trade partners to engage in recreational sex. It publishes a newsletter, *EMERGE Playcouple.* The organization also sponsors a yearly Erotic Masquerade Ball.

Morality in Media, Inc. (MIM)
475 Riverside Drive
New York, NY 10115
(212) 870-3222

MIM believes pornography corrupts children and degrades both men and women. It has worked since 1962 to alert citizens to the dangers of pornography and to demand that the courts enforce obscenity laws. It publishes the *Handbook on the Prosecution of Obscenity Cases* and a bimonthly newsletter.

National Center for Lesbian Rights Project
1370 Mission St., 4th Floor
San Francisco, CA 94103
(415) 621-0674

The Project is a public interest law office providing legal counseling and representation for victims of sexual orientation discrimination. Primary areas of advice are in custody and parenting, employment, housing, the military, and insurance. The Project also publishes *The Lesbian Mother Litigation Manual* and *Lesbians Choose Motherhood: Legal Issues in Donor Insemination* as well as a bibliography on lesbian mothers and children.

National Coalition Against Pornography (N-CAP)
800 Compton Rd., Suite 9224
Cincinnati, OH 45231-9964
(513) 521-6227

N-CAP is an organization of business, religious, and civic leaders who work to eliminate pornography. They use the media to convince Americans that there is a link between pornography and violence. They encourage citizens to support the enforcement of obscenity laws and to close down pornography outlets in their neighborhoods. Their publications include *Final Report of the Attorney General's Commission on Pornography, The Mind Polluters,* and *Pornography: A Human Tragedy.*

National Gay and Lesbian Crisis Line
Fund for Human Dignity
666 Broadway, 4th Floor
New York, NY 10012
(212) 529-1600
1-800-767-4297 (hotline)

The Crisis Line is a project of the Fund for Human Dignity, an organization dedicated to educating the public about the lives of homosexuals. The Crisis Line offers information on gay and lesbian issues as well as on AIDS. The Fund publishes the *National AIDS Resource Directory* and the quarterly *Fund Focus*.

National Gay and Lesbian Task Force (NGLTF)
1517 U St. NW
Washington, DC 20009
(202) 332-6483

NGLTF works to eliminate prejudice on the basis of sexual orientation. It lobbies for gay civil rights and for the reform of laws that make sodomy illegal in many states. NGLTF distributes *Dealing with Violence: A Guide for Gay and Lesbian People*; *Hardwick, Sodomy Laws, and Our Fight for Sexual Freedom*; and *AIDS-Related Issues and Insurance*, as well as many other pamphlets.

Planned Parenthood
810 7th Ave.
New York, NY 10019
(212) 541-7800

Planned Parenthood believes people should make their own decisions about having children. They support sex education and provide contraceptive counseling and services through clinics located throughout the United States. Among their extensive publications are the quarterly *Review*, and the brochures *Guide to Birth Control: Seven Accepted Methods of Contraception*; *Teensex? It's OK To Say No Way*; *A Man's Guide to Sexuality*; and *About Childbirth*.

Sex Information and Education Council of the US (SIECUS)
80 5th Ave., Suite 801
New York, NY 10011
(212) 929-2300

SIECUS is one of the largest national clearinghouses for information on sexuality. The Council reviews books on human sexuality and compiles annotated bibliographies of sex education resources. They also publish a newsletter, *SIECUS Report*, and books, including *Winning the Battle for Sex Education*, *Adolescent Pregnancy, and Parenthood*, and *Media and Sexuality/Sex Education*.

Womanity
1700 Oak Park Blvd.
Pleasant Hill, CA 94523
(415) 943-6424

Womanity is an organization of Christian feminist laywomen who are pro-chastity, pro-life, and anti-pornography. They oppose permissive sex and narcissistic self-fulfillment. Womanity publishes several flyers, including *Sex Appreciation: A Handbook on Chastity*, *How To Say No*, and *Gone All the Way—Now Where?* They also distribute the videotapes *Just Wait* and *Saving Sex for Marriage*.

Women Against Pornography (WAP)
358 W. 47th St.
New York, NY 10036
(212) 307-5055

WAP was founded by Susan Brownmiller, the feminist author of *Against Our Will: Men, Women, and Rape*. WAP works to change public attitudes toward pornography by offering tours of Times Square, New York's porn center, and by offering slide shows for adults and high school students which show how pornography brutalizes women. They publish a quarterly newsletter.

Bibliography of Books

Isobel Allen   *Education in Sex and Personal Relationships*. London: Policy Studies Institute, 1987.

David Bertelson   *Snowflakes and Snowdrifts: Individualism and Sexuality in America*. Lanham, MD: University Press of America, 1986.

A.R. Cavaliere, ed.   *Selected Topics in Human Sexuality*. Lanham, MD: University Press of America, 1988.

David Chilton   *Power in the Blood: A Christian Response to AIDS*. Brentwood, TN: Woglemuth and Hyatt Publishers, 1987.

Nancy Compton, Mara Duncan, and Jack Hruska   *How Schools Can Help Combat Student Pregnancy*. Washington, DC: National Education Association, 1987.

Edward Donnerstein, Daniel Linz, and Stephen Penrod   *The Question of Pornography: Research Findings and Policy Implications*. New York: Free Press, 1987.

Jack D. Douglas and Freda Cruise Atwell   *Love, Intimacy, and Sex*. Newbury Park, CA: Sage Publications, Inc., 1988.

William H. DuBay   *Gay Identity: The Self Under Ban*. Jefferson, NC: McFarland & Co., Inc., 1987.

Andrea Dworkin   *Intercourse*. New York: Free Press, 1987.

Richard C. Friedman   *Male Homosexuality: A Contemporary Psychoanalytic Perspective*. New Haven, CT: Yale University Press, 1988.

Richard Green   *The "Sissy Boy Syndrome."* New Haven, CT: Yale University Press, 1987.

David F. Greenberg   *The Construction of Homosexuality*. Chicago: The University of Chicago Press, 1988.

James P. Hanigan   *Homosexuality: The Test Case for Christian Sexual Ethics*. New York: Paulist Press, 1988.

Gordon Hawkins and Franklin E. Zimring   *Pornography in a Free Society*. New York: Cambridge University Press, 1988.

John Huer   *Art, Beauty, and Pornography*. Buffalo, NY: Prometheus Books, 1987.

Fred Isbener   *Sex Education in a Church Setting*. Carbondale, IL: Southern Illinois University Press, 1987.

Morton Kelsey and Barbara Kelsey   *Sacrament of Sexuality: The Spirituality and Psychology of Sex*. Warwick, NY: Amity House, 1986.

Walter Kendrick   *The Secret Museum: Pornography in Modern Culture*. New York: Viking Press, 1987.

Philip E. Lampe, ed.   *Adultery in the United States*. Buffalo, NY: Prometheus Books, 1987.

George Leonard   *Adventures in Monogamy*. Los Angeles: Jeremy P. Tarcher, Inc., 1988.

Catharine A. MacKinnon | *Feminism Unmodified*. Cambridge, MA: Harvard University Press, 1987.

Lawrence J. McNamee and Brian F. McNamee | *AIDS: The Nation's First Politically Protected Disease*. La Habra, CA: National Medical Legal Publishing House, 1988.

Connaught Marshner | *Decent Exposure: How To Teach Your Children About Sex*. Brentwood, TN: Woglemuth and Hyatt Publishers, 1988.

William H. Masters, Virginia E. Johnson, and Robert C. Kolodny | *Crisis: Heterosexual Behavior in the Age of AIDS*. New York: Grove Press, 1988.

William H. Masters, Virginia E. Johnson, and Robert C. Kolodny | *Masters and Johnson on Sex and Human Loving*. Boston: Little, Brown and Company, 1986.

Paul A. Mickey | *Sex with Confidence*. New York: William Morrow and Company, Inc., 1988.

Richard D. Mohr | *Gays/Justice*. New York: Columbia University Press, 1988.

Barrett L. Mosbacker, ed. | *School-Based Clinics and Other Critical Issues in Public Education*. Westchester, IL: Crossway Books, 1987.

Sandra Pollack and Jeanne Vaughn, eds. | *Politics of the Heart: A Lesbian Parenting Anthology*. Ithaca, NY: Firebrand Books, 1987.

Laurel Richardson and Verta Taylor | *Feminist Frontiers II: Rethinking Sex, Gender, and Society*. New York: Random House, 1989.

Ines Rieder and Patricia Ruppelt, eds. | *AIDS: The Women*. San Francisco: Cleis Press, 1989.

Enrique T. Rueda and Michael Schwartz | *Gays, AIDS, and You*. Old Greenwich, CT: Devin Adair Co., 1987.

Edwin M. Schur | *The Americanization of Sex*. Philadelphia: Temple University Press, 1988.

Randy Shilts | *And the Band Played On: Politics, People, and the AIDS Epidemic*. New York: St. Martin's Press, 1987.

Susan Sontag | *AIDS and Its Metaphors*. New York: Farrar, Straus, Giroux, 1989.

Ernie Zimbelman | *Human Sexuality and Evangelical Christians*. Lanham, MD: University Press of America, 1985.

Index